AF255966

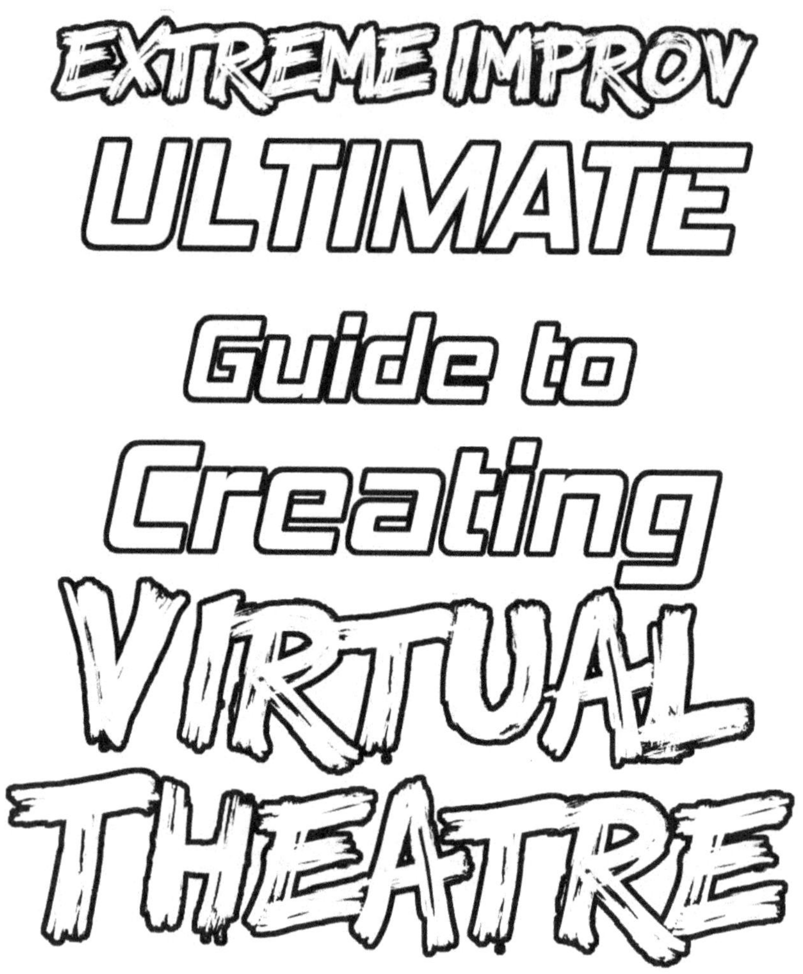

DAVID PUSTANSKY

Extreme Improv Ultimate Guide to Creating Virtual Theatre

by David Pustansky

Copyright © David Pustansky 2022

All rights reserved.

Published by Extreme Improv

www.xstreamed.tv

www.extremeimprov.co.uk

www.geekbattle.tv

First published in 2022

extremeimprovcomedy@gmail.com

Featuring artwork and photography by David Pustansky

Paperback ISBN:

Ebook ISBN:

10 9 8 7 6 5 4 3 2 1

First Edition

i: JOIN THE EXTREME IMPROV COMMUNITY

Extreme Improv Xstreamed welcomes you to join our growing community and to get involved!

Here at Extreme Improv, we welcome performers from all over the world and from all backgrounds and experience levels to get involved and take part in our projects.

We create hilarious live in person shows that perform in theatres, run in person workshops, and are one of the most prolific producers of virtual improv shows in the world. We're always happy to hear from new people who'd like to get involved, so get in touch!

To get involved, you can either contact us through our main website

www.xstreamed.tv

or connect with us through our social media channels.

Facebook page

www.facebook.com/extremeimprov

Join our Facebook community group where we post weekly show sign ups

www.facebook.com/groups/extremeimprovxstreamed/

Twitter

www.twitter.com/extremeimprov

Check out our shows on the Extreme Improv XStreamed YouTube Channel

www.youtube.com/extremeimprov

Instagram

www.instagram.com/extremeimprov

TikTok

www.tiktok.com/@extremeimprov

ii: SUPPORT THE EXTREME IMPROV XSTREAMED ONLINE CHANNEL

This book is all about creating online shows and content, and Extreme Improv create a ton of shows and other online content!

Please subscribe to the Extreme Improv XStreamed YouTube Channel!

If you'd like to support our virtual theatre shows, the number one way you can do it is by heading over to the Extreme Improv YouTube channel and clicking the red subscribe button! Anyone with a YouTube/Gmail account can do it and it's completely free!

The more subscribers we get on the channel, the more YouTube will recommend our virtual theatre shows to other YouTube users. So, if you can, please subscribe and share our shows with others to help Extreme Improv and virtual theatre grow!

www.youtube.com/extremeimprov

Here's an overview of some of the virtual shows we create!

- Extreme Improv XStreamed: Short form improv show
- Geek Battle: Comedy panel show based on geek culture
- Slam Jam Wrestling Show: Comedy panel show based on pro wrestling
- Extreme Improv Revenge: Long form social deduction improv show
- XStreamed Jesters Jam: Quick fire joke telling improv gameshow
- Totally Sketchy: Art based gameshow
- Wham Bam Poetry Slam: Poetry based improv gameshow

Virtual Theatre Festivals

We also create online virtual theatre festivals including

- The Extreme Improv XStreamed World Championship
- The Extreme Improv XStreamed Team Championship
- Virtually Unstoppable Theatre Festival

TABLE OF CONTENTS

1: INTRODUCTION

Welcome to the Extreme Improv Ultimate Guide to Creating Virtual Theatre! I very much hope that you find this guide useful, as I've written it to help give ideas, guides, tips and tricks for virtual theatre producers and performers of all experience levels.

Virtual theatre is an art form which is very new, and it's very exciting. It's an artform so new, in fact, that even the name 'virtual theatre' isn't completely agreed upon. Online theatre, Zoom Theatre, internet television and a range of other terms have all been used to describe this performance type, but I'll stick with the term virtual theatre for now.

Virtual theatre has only been around in any significant way for a couple of years at the time of writing, and people are still trying to figure much of it out. There isn't a Hollywood or other authority on virtual theatre. There are no drama schools or film schools that specialise in virtual theatre. Virtual theatre is still finding its place in the world of performing arts.

We can trace the origins of theatre back as far as Ancient Greece, over two and a half thousand years ago. There has been huge amounts of evolution and innovation since the time of Thespis, the first actor.

What started with open air performances and poetry readings at the Theatre of Dionysus has evolved throughout history to the amphitheatres of Rome, medieval plays, Shakespeare and the Globe Theatre, all the way through to modern times where now we have the West End and Broadway, radio, cinema and television, and even the ability to watch clips of Friends and Breaking Bad on TikTok whilst sat on the toilet...

OK, so I took a sharp turn at the end there for comedic effect, but the point is that where we are at now is born of thousands of years of evolution and refinement. Recorded mediums of radio, cinema and television are still relatively new in comparison, with the first radio and television broadcasts only happening around a hundred years ago.

When you consider that early films were black and white, silent, and generally shot from a distance like you were filming a wide shot of a stage…because camera angles hadn't been invented yet, you can see that things have come a long way. Now we have drone cameras, CGI, and physical sets being replaced by giant screens that display cities or alien worlds created in unreal engine.

This brings me back to virtual theatre, which has only really existed since 2020 when the COVID-19 pandemic put most of the world into lockdown, and creative people turned to their computers to keep the spirit of theatre and performance alive.

In its very short history, virtual theatre exploded into popularity out of necessity, people scrambled to figure out how to do it, and they innovated with what can be achieved online. Like all new artforms and technology, many people embraced it, whilst others completely shunned it, seeing it as inferior, or pointless, a fad, or worst of all, damaging to other areas of the performing arts industry.

I don't see virtual theatre as a negative at all. It's new, and that alone is enough to make it exciting. I'll never be able to go back in time and be part of the invention of the basic plot types of comedy and tragedy. The Ancient Greeks handled that without me. Nor will I be able to able to go back to 1902 and take part in the filming of Le Voyage dans la Lune, and shape the future of science fiction cinema.

What I can do, and what I hope this book will help you, the reader, to do, is be part of the development of this new branch of performing arts known as virtual theatre. I run the improvised theatre company Extreme Improv, and its related brand Xstreamed.tv and since 2018, even before the pandemic started, I have been working on translating our improv comedy shows to online formats. Firstly where we'd adapt the performance to an online show, filmed with cast and crew all in one physical location, and also where cast would meet virtually over Skype.

When the pandemic hit the UK in March 2020, I was amongst the first batch of virtual theatre producers to start creating regular online shows. I quickly decided that presentation and production values would be a focus of what I'd create, and I also quickly found an appreciation for the benefits that virtual theatre had to offer. Shows could be put together quickly, cast and audience could come from all over the world, and I found that cost wise, I was able to produce hundreds of shows for the same expense of one or two in person shows.

In the time since I began creating virtual theatre, I have had a keen interest in seeing what is possible with online performances, and whilst many have taken a step back from virtual theatre since the lockdowns have ended, I'm all the more excited to delve deeper into it. At the time of writing I have produced close to 1,000 virtual shows, and have written this book to help others discover or rediscover everything that is great about virtual theatre.

I've spent months trying every piece of video meeting and broadcasting software under the sun, and have written guides for all the major software that you will need to create a brilliant virtual theatre show. I've explored which software is worth using, and discovered which isn't worth using, and done this work so you don't have to. And despite some of the software not being ideal, or some being downright difficult to use for creating virtual theatre shows, I have written guides for them anyway.

I'm aware that computer software, hardware and technology in general will continue to evolve, and within time some of this book will become outdated. As such, I've tried to make my guides as universally relevant as possible, so even when software changes, the ideas of what you'll want to create in a show will still be useful to read about.

I've also included detailed tips and guides for how to run a virtual theatre show as a technician, or how to perform in virtual theatre shows as an actor. I've also included other useful things like how to build an audience and ideas for ways to make money with virtual theatre.

I'll wrap up this introduction now, but hope you are just as excited for your journey into the world of virtual theatre as I am, and hope you have fun with the Extreme Improv Ultimate Guide to Virtual Theatre!

2: ABOUT THE AUTHOR

My name is David Pustansky. I do lots of different things, but primarily I'm an actor, comedian, writer and a director, and I run the improvised comedy show Extreme Improv XStreamed and its related brand and website www.xstreamed.tv

I trained professionally as an actor at a drama school in London, and most of my career has been working in the performing arts and entertainment industry. I have appeared in films, commercials, plays, podcasts, and everything in between.

I have a huge passion for creating projects and have dabbled in tons of different creative areas. This has included creating traditional hand drawn animated films, recording and releasing songs, doing graffiti art as set design on theatre productions and creating custom computer software and video games. I sometimes think of myself as a Jack of all trades and a master of none but feel that learning a range of different skills enables me to be better at each one.

One area I didn't think I would get into as much as I have is writing. I've always enjoyed writing, and have written lots of plays and short films. I love the storytelling aspect of it, but I didn't imagine a few years ago that I'd ever write books. This book that you're reading now is my second book. My first book was the Extreme Improv Big Book of Improv Games which was released in mid 2020. It was a guide on how to play over a hundred short form improv games, and aimed as a useful guide for performers, directors, teachers, or anyone who just wanted to have fun doing improv.

Having written the first book, I was keen to write more, and it led to me creating the website www.xstreamed.tv The website allowed me a place to not only share things about Extreme Improv, but also as a place to create content about all kinds of things that interest me. This includes articles and videos about travel, movies, food, video games, sport, and now I find that whenever I'm not performing or working on shows, I'm writing.

One of the thoughts I had when writing my first book was that I wanted to spread the word about improv and help it reach more people. Not because I saw it as a cause or quest, but because I love doing improv, and I had the realisation that despite considerable growth in the last few years, improv is still fairly niche. I wanted more people to be on the same page with it as I am because then I'd have more people to do it with.

The same thought process applies with this book on virtual theatre. Since discovering virtual theatre, I think it's a fantastic and creative outlet, which can help showcase talent, connect people around the world and is easy to get into...but tricky to master.

3: ABOUT EXTREME IMPROV XSTREAMED

Extreme Improv began life in 2010. I started it whilst training at drama school, but at the time it was known as The ImProDigies Theatre Company…and yes for some reason I stylised the name that way…

For a few years I would do sporadic improv shows here and there, but as I found I was doing more things that were scripted, and filmed projects that weren't theatre, the name ImProDigies Theatre Company didn't feel it made sense. So, I renamed it Sparky Buddy Productions!

To explain that name, I had a budgie named Sparky and a dog called Buddy. I also liked that the term Sparky Buddy meant bright and intelligent friend. Sparky Buddy Productions released a bunch of short films, and produced plays which performed at various venues across the UK. Even though I was doing other stuff, I hadn't given up on improv. Far from it.

In 2017 I created a new improv show that was intended to be a one off show idea. That show was called Extreme Championship Improv, and the idea was that it would be improv mixed with a pro wrestling style presentation. It was a competitive show, and the winner would get to hold up a championship belt at the end. People really liked the show, and cast and audience both wanted to do more.

So Extreme Championship Improv continued with more shows into early 2018, but for all my work to build up the Sparky Buddy Productions name, people just started calling the company Extreme Improv…or to be more precise, the Extreme Improv Championship…which was wrong, but in fairness to them, it was what I called the championship belt. Realising that I had gone full circle back to improv I decided that Extreme Improv would be the improv theatre company section of Sparky Buddy Productions.

Extreme Improv would have live comedy shows all over the UK and I started taking my improvised show to venues and festivals in the United States, Japan, Europe, and even started online shows, although these were pre-recorded and not streamed live.

The pandemic hit in 2020, and as we'll get into later in this book, the virtual theatre era of Extreme Improv XStreamed began.

To explain the company name for a fourth time in this one section…I announced the Extreme Improv online show would be called Extreme Improv Streamlined, as I wanted a clever name to reflect that the show would be live streamed on the internet. Then one day later I realised that 'stream' as in live stream sounded exactly like the second syllable of the word 'extreme' which was already the show name. So rather than say Extreme Improv Streamed, I added an X (because the letter X makes everything more cool) and it became Extreme Improv XStreamed!

As well as producing multiple short form Extreme Improv XStreamed shows each week, I also created other shows such as Extreme Improv Revenge, Geek Battle and Slam Jam.

History was repeating again. These weren't all strictly improv. Geek Battle and Slam Jam are comedy panel shows themed on geek culture and wrestling respectively. They aren't strictly improv shows…but they are streaming…So I decided to lean further into the XStreamed name, and I created a brand and website just called Xstreamed.tv

It's crazy that in writing this history of Extreme Improv, I've been able to focus on four or five brand renames, but the names reflect the evolution of the company.

Extreme Improv XStreamed as it is today produces all kinds of content, from the Jet Lagged and Loving It travel vlog, to live Extreme Improv comedy shows on stages around the world, to Geek Battle and Geek Battle Gaming content based on movies and gaming. I've created Extreme Improv XStreamed books, board games, mobile apps and a heck of a lot of virtual theatre shows. Here's to whatever comes next!

4: WHAT IS VIRTUAL THEATRE?

Virtual theatre is the broad term given to the types of performance that are done using webcams and streamed over the internet. It can cover plays, musicals, stand up, improv, children's theatre, dance, sketch comedy and pretty much anything which could be performed on stage.

Virtual theatre came to prominence during the COVID-19 worldwide pandemic and really took off in 2020 as the solution to in person shows and cinemas being closed to the public. During this time, virtual theatre provided a way for performers to keep creative, and both performers and audiences to keep a sense of community and connection with one another.

People all over the world would connect to each other via their computers and smart phones to engage in the performing arts. It was a great demonstration of how the arts communities were able to adapt and keep going in the face of the restrictions of lockdown.

The pandemic was a terrible time of suffering and uncertainty, and changed many things in the world which may last forever. Concepts of social distancing and PPE were not widely known before the pandemic but are now firmly baked into the minds of everyone on the planet. Paying by card instead of using cash, home deliveries and video calls are now also much more common as a result of the pandemic.

History has taught us that most things that can move towards technology will eventually do so, and the pandemic accelerated this. In the case of virtual theatre, the leap towards technology was gigantic and probably accelerated what may have otherwise taken 10 years.

Virtual theatre didn't start with the pandemic as companies have been dabbling with live and pre-recorded shows that are designed with an internet audience in mind for as long as the internet has existed. Though they are not quite the same as what people would now consider virtual theatre, podcasts, radio plays, and even gaming and 'just chatting' live streams all existed before the pandemic and were in one way or another a form of virtual theatre.

At the time of writing, most virtual theatre is performed over Zoom or via similar video conferencing software. Performers set up stationary cameras and talk towards their screens. In many ways the artform is like an evolved radio play, where locations, props and physical interaction primarily exists in the mind's eye of the audience. Performers are usually presented in mid to close up shots and shown in a grid onscreen on shows being streamed to platforms like YouTube and Facebook.

In the future, virtual or augmented reality may allow our performances to be represented with realistic avatars which we control like video game characters with motion capture technology.

The virtual reality Holodeck of Star Trek seems like impossible science fiction today, but in the 1960s, the communicators used by Captain Kirk and Spock also seemed impossible. Those same communicators now seem very outdated compared to the smart phones which everyone has today, so who knows what the future will bring.

Virtual theatre will probably never fully replace in person theatre, and I wouldn't want it to, but it can sit alongside it as an alternative and compliment it to allow for more performance opportunities overall.

5: THE BENEFITS OF VIRTUAL THEATRE VS TRADITIONAL THEATRE

Virtual theatre isn't the same as live in person theatre. There are lots of things which are the same between the two forms of theatre, but there are many many differences. Some of these are good differences, and some of these are bad differences.

As we'll discuss many times throughout the book, some of the drawbacks of virtual theatre include the lack of physical interaction between performers that you can do online, and that there can be many tech issues that you wouldn't face on stage. You'll face other challenges on stage, but you're not likely to have the issue that a performer vanishes because their Wi-Fi went down!

But enough of the negatives for a moment, as we'll cover the challenges of virtual theatre continually throughout the book and provide ideas for solutions for them. For now, let's look at the positives and benefits of virtual theatre, because there are many. If you haven't considered all of these, they may help you decide to take the plunge or dive back into the world of virtual theatre.

The cost

I can't put this one over enough. Generally speaking, the cost of producing virtual theatre can be next to nothing compared to the costs of creating an in person show. Certainly, there can be many costs involved with virtual theatre, and this can include equipment, subscriptions to software and services to stream shows, but let's break down the differences a bit more here.

If you're doing an in person show, every cast and team member will have had to arrive in person to a performance or rehearsal venue at the same time. This takes a lot of coordination of schedules, and unless everyone is within walking distance of the venue, you'll all have costs of fuel, buses, taxis, trains etc etc. Also, unless you're lucky to have a venue you can work at for free, you'll have to hire a space somewhere.

On top of venue costs, in person shows may require vehicle hire for touring, set design, technicians, costume and props and the list goes on and on and on. Producing theatre, even small-scale theatre can quickly become a very expensive endeavour.

And yes, I'm aware that on the flip side you could say that everyone who wants to do virtual theatre needs a computer or smartphone, but realistically, most people who would do in person theatre would have access to these.

Virtual theatre eliminates many of the costs of in person theatre entirely. People can perform from anywhere they can get an internet signal, which makes scheduling people easier. You can still use props, sets, and costumes for virtual theatre, but the expectations of the audience are very different and there is so much which can be effectively achieved using green screens or filters from the comfort of your own home.

Schedule

As mentioned already, it's much easier to schedule people to meet virtually than it is to do so with people in person. If a performer is 45 minutes away from a rehearsal venue that means they need to set aside 90 additional minutes in travel in addition to the actual rehearsal time. If people have other jobs or family commitments this extra time may mean they struggle to commit to a project.

Jumping onto a video meeting can be done from almost anywhere. If someone can only join for a few minutes because of a conflict in their schedule, it's a lot easier to make a video meeting work than it is to ask someone to travel a distance for just a few minutes of in person time.

You can access cast from all over the world

A great thing about virtual theatre is that it can bring people and cultures from all over the planet together to work and play together. You could have a show that has five people in it, and each of them could be in a different country and time zone. Bringing that exact cast together in real life may never be possible due to cost and logistics.

Being able to work with a diverse cast from different backgrounds and cultures can really expand everyone's knowledge of different working practices. Things you may do out of habit may be different or new to other countries, and this includes their style, presentation and even tech.

Audience can join from all over the world too

Just as you can have performers from all over the world, a great benefit for any actors and producers out there is that it has never been easier to get your work seen by a worldwide audience.

Whether its YouTube or another platform, people can watch live or watch later from anywhere.

Accessibility

A benefit that isn't spoken about enough is that virtual theatre makes the arts accessible for many people who may not be able to access or take part otherwise.

It has opened the doors for people who live in remote areas where there is little or no opportunity to take part in the performing arts to get involved. It also gives a way for people with a huge range of health conditions, who may otherwise not be able to take part, to join in and enjoy the performing arts.

You don't have to deal with venues

Theatre makers will know that it can sometimes be a challenge to deal with venues at times. You may want to produce a show at a particular venue which is unavailable when you'd like it, or you may find that the venue may not book you. You will also need to be aware of things specific to each venue such as rules, timings, space size and lots more.

If you're streaming on your own personal social media page, you effectively are your own venue, and you don't have to deal with these kinds of headaches that can exist in the real world.

Last minute changes and delays don't mean that much online

In an ideal world, you'll plan your show, and nothing will go wrong. But we don't live in an ideal world. Therefore, actors have understudies, and we keep spare lightbulbs and mics in case things break.

For a performance in real life, if an actor falls sick, or misses their train, you may need an understudy to jump in. You may even have a few understudies in case something unfortunate happens with several performers. In the virtual world, you can quickly access anyone on your contacts list to jump on a video call last minute.

Certainly, if you're doing something scripted, or heavily rehearsed, you may not have tons of people who can fill in if they don't know your show. If, however, the performer can get away with reading a script, or improvising, the potential pool of performers you can call upon at short notice is any performer with access to an internet connection.

If a stand-up comic or improviser drops out last minute, you no longer have to worry about 'who can get here in the next hour?' Because anyone from across the world could step in and step up.

Likewise, a major technical difficulty in a virtual show isn't always as problematic as a technical difficulty in an in person show. People can perform in or watch virtual shows from anywhere, so if you need to delay a show by 15 minutes whilst you solve issues, you can easily do so. Even if you started an online show an hour late it's not like audiences would panic that they'll miss the last train home because they can watch from anywhere.

Of course, by this same token, there are scenarios where in person theatre has advantages. As long as all the cast are at a venue, a performance could theoretically continue in the spirit of 'the show must go on' even if mics broke, lights burnt out and they cast had to perform lit only by flashlights and candles. A virtual show can't survive if there is a power outage for the person streaming the show.

Marketing is much easier and cost effectively... broadly speaking

Marketing a virtual theatre show can be as simple as sharing or sending people the web address for where they will watch your show online. And your potential audience is anyone who can access the internet to watch it from anywhere around the world.

An in-person show can also be marketed online, but who you can realistically expect to show up to your event is going to be heavily restricted to a geographical area. This instantly makes your potential audience tiny compared to the potential audience you can get online.

With an online show, there is no upper limit to how many people can watch live, and you also have the added benefit that people can watch on demand in their own time later. A live show will have the limit of how many people can fit into the venue, and this adds pressure to fill as many seats as possible so that no seat is left unused.

This pressure to 'sell out' a venue can lead to greater expense, because if you don't do all you can and the show doesn't sell out, there is always that feeling that 'you could have done more'. The 'more' that you could do usually includes paying for flyers, posters, roller banners and other physical marketing materials which certainly are useful alongside an online marketing campaign, but come at added cost. These materials then need distributing and that is a lot of time/expense as well.

Certainly, you could get flyers printed for an online show, but with an online show this doesn't make as much sense. With a potential worldwide audience, where would you choose to send physical flyers for an online show? And why there and not to another town, or country? Unless you're planning to get 7 billion flyers made for everyone on Earth, it's easier to keep to online marketing for an online show.

6: A NOTE ABOUT TECHNOLOGY

In this book, I will at times talk about specific equipment and software that can be used, and at other times I'll speak more broadly.

I have included detailed guides on how to create shows with various pieces of software that are current at the time of writing.

Because technology is always improving and evolving, I am aware that some of the things that I cover in this book may be hilariously outdated by the time you read it. As such, I'll endeavour to talk broadly enough so you can continue to apply the ideas discussed to whatever are the latest cameras, microphones, software etc.

A final note about the technology covered in this book is that I approach it as a Windows PC user. Whilst I know that much of what I say will apply to Mac users as well, there may be some differences to what software is available and how it works if you use a different operating system.

Likewise, I am primarily an iPhone/iPad user when it comes to smart devices, although I do have and frequently use Android based phones and tablets as well.

7: BEFORE YOU BEGIN – DO YOU HAVE YOUR SHOW?

One of the first things you'll discover when you try to create an online show is that the process of making an online show, and the end result, is quite different from a live stage show. Some things just need minor tweaks, but there will be things that need big alterations.

Do you know what your show is going to be? In this guide, I'll go over lots of things for you to think about, but without knowing your show, you'll have to take these ideas and fill in the blanks.

If you have an idea for a show that was initially designed as a concept for stage, be prepared to make adjustments to adapt it for a virtual theatre performance.

If on the other hand, you are approaching this book as the starting point, we'll go over what is and isn't a good fit in terms of virtual theatre. The great thing about designing a virtual show from the ground up is that you can concentrate on the strengths of what lends itself to online performance, and minimise the things that aren't a great fit for the medium.

Do you have a cast and crew? Are they tech ready?

A big consideration when putting together a virtual theatre performance will be making sure that everyone involved is tech ready. Later in this guide we'll cover varying levels of tech that can be used to enhance your show, and even considerations for how to perform virtually (Chapter 23), but making sure everyone involved understands what you're trying to achieve is essential to making the best show possible.

If your cast isn't very capable with the tech involved, you'll benefit from having your technician/director/producer play around with the various pieces of software that you'll need to use. The more familiar you are with the tech, the easier it will be to help the less tech savvy cast get up to speed with what they may need to know.

The good news is that to get basic results, the tech required and entry skill level is low. After all, many people have gotten used to video calls for work, education or socialising. But the more familiar you are with the tech, the further you'll be able to take your show beyond the basic to create impressive and advanced virtual shows.

As more and more people become familiar with the tech and skills involved in virtual performance it will be easier to put out castings for people who are already competent performing virtually. If you have a pre-established cast, the challenge will be in making sure everyone can learn the new skills required.

For some, the concept of performing virtually will not be their cup of tea. Throughout the early years of virtual performance in the COVID-19 pandemic, there were many who grew tired of the format, and many who chose not to participate in the first place.

The thought I'd give to any performers who are unsure, or not keen to take part virtually, is that it is a new type of performance, and that it offers many positives as discussed in chapter 5. I'd also remind them that as a performance medium in its infancy, there will be a period of getting used to it and learning how to make the most of it.

If ultimately you find performers you have previously worked with are not keen to take part in virtual shows, this will be the opportunity to seek fresh blood. This is a new performance medium, and it's exciting to think that those who take it up now will be the pioneers who will shape what exactly virtual theatre becomes in the future.

Just as silent films started the revolution that is today's cinema, and the early filmmakers and actors had to figure out the tech and how to perform for it, so too do today's generation of creatives and actors need to develop virtual theatre for future generations.

8: BEFORE YOU BEGIN – WHAT EQUIPMENT YOU'LL NEED

Ok, we're past the introductory chapters. It's time to get serious. If you want to make virtual theatre shows, you'll need some equipment. This is where things can start to sound expensive, but the reality is that most people will be able to get started with a phone that they already have in their pocket, or with a laptop they already own. Lots of the software that is useful is free, or has free options.

It is true that you get what you pay for, and the more money and higher quality equipment you use, the better the results can be. So, let's dig into what you'll need to make the best virtual theatre shows at various budget levels.

An internet connection

When it comes to internet access there are two main routes.

Option 1: Internet through a router. The type found in most homes or businesses.

Option 2: Mobile internet from a smart device such as a phone or tablet.

The quick answer to which will give you the most stable internet is option 1, but both have advantages, so let's break them down one at a time.

Internet through a router

As obvious as it sounds, without a way to connect to the internet you will not be creating a virtual theatre performance. Internet through a router will give you a more consistent stable connection than attempting to stream just via a mobile/cellular phone. With mobile, depending on where you are streaming from, you may enter a dead zone where there is little or no internet signal. If you've had an internet service provider set up Wi-fi in your home and it doesn't work, you're within your right to get them back out to fix it, as a stable internet connection within the radius of your home is what you're paying them for.

There are many internet service providers, and you'll have to research what companies offer in your area, but you'll want the fastest internet connection possible.

The most important thing to consider is 'Upload speed'. This is essential for streaming high-quality footage out over the internet. It's important that you don't muddle up upload speed with download speed.

Download speed will dictate how quickly you can download data, such as downloading a game, or watching Netflix without it buffering. Upload speeds are never as fast as the download speed, and you need to be careful to make sure you get a fast upload speed as that will dictate what quality footage you can broadcast.

If you can't afford the fastest internet speeds, you'll either find that your high-quality footage doesn't display well or that your stream crashes often. You could always start with lower speeds and upgrade when you become more comfortable with creating virtual theatre. To accommodate for lower speeds, you'd be best off lowering the graphical settings of your streams so it's not a heavy load, but we'll cover that more later in chapter 14.

High level: Get the fastest internet you can afford. This will allow you to stream out high quality footage and have the least chance of streams crashing.

Mid level: If you can't afford the fastest internet, just get what you can afford, but you'll need to make sure settings are lowered. For example, if your settings were for 4K or Full HD footage, you may have to lower this so that your internet doesn't crash out on you.

Low level: You'll definitely need to lower your quality settings to accommodate for a slower connection speed. This will mean that your video will have a lower resolution, but you'll have the best chance of avoiding the stream cutting out.

Other considerations:

Wi-fi vs Ethernet and your router

If you get your internet at home, you can explore what router to use. The router is the device that you'll have in your home that gives the internet signal to your house. The better the router you have, the more stable your signal will be. Your internet service provider will give you a router when they install your internet, although you could purchase a higher quality one that may increase the speed or reach of your internet.

The best advice I can give on this one is to find a router designed for gamers. Gamers who stream gameplay footage will use many of the same devices as needed for virtual theatre, so if you are also interested in streaming video games, much of this will apply for that as well.

Once you have your router set up, you'll need to decide if you want a wired or wireless internet connection. Without question, a wired connection via an Ethernet cable is superior to a Wi-Fi connection. Depending on where you have your streaming area set up in your house, using a wired connection may or may not be possible, but for the best results, always use an Ethernet cable.

If you can't use an Ethernet cable, you could consider using a Wi-Fi boosting device, as this will improve the signal, but isn't as stable as wired.

Internet via a smart device such a mobile/cellular phone or tablet

You can use your phone/tablet to connect to the internet if you have a mobile data plan, and this can also be used as a hotspot to connect your computer/laptop to the internet.

This can be a good alternative if your home internet is experiencing technical issues, or if you want to create shows away from your home internet connection. Using your phone/tablet as a hotspot generally won't match the reliability of a Wi-Fi/Ethernet connection.

The biggest benefit of using your phone/tablet's SIM card to stream from is that you can do it from anywhere you are able to get a signal. This is great for performers as it means that you can easily take part in shows from pretty much anywhere and will provide you with many more opportunities to perform.

For producers of shows, I'd give the slight warning that whilst it is still very possible to stream from anywhere, you will have more considerations than if you were just performing.

There are many things that you cannot currently achieve from the software/hardware available on phones/tablets. If you plan to use just your phone/tablet to produce shows you should be ok for much of the time, but many of the more advanced things we'll discuss would require the use of a computer/laptop to run the show. In this case, your phone/tablet would just be used as a mobile hotspot to connect to the internet.

Using your phone/tablet as a hotspot for your laptop is doable, but depending how many bells and whistles you add, and what resolution the footage is, you may find your phone internet doesn't cope well.

The most important consideration in doing virtual theatre from your phone/tablet is the cost/how much internet data you have to play with each month.

If you have a low data plan, you can forget streaming via your smart device's mobile data. You don't want to be halfway through a show and suddenly find you disconnect, or worse still, that you are running up a huge bill.

My experience

I'm in the UK, and currently use the mobile provider Three, and have done so for several years, because they have offered truly unlimited internet access. This isn't to say they have offered the best service, or that there aren't others who offer a more stable connection, but as of the time of writing, they're the only one that offers truly unlimited amounts of data use.

Many others say they offer unlimited data, but in the fine print they usually mention a data cap, so in other words, it's not actually unlimited.

I got the unlimited data option long before virtual theatre became a thing, and I did it so that I wouldn't worry about streaming the likes of YouTube or Netflix. I have found it useful for my virtual theatre needs on occasion, although primarily as a performer, and not as a producer. As a performer, I have done a few shows whilst away from my home internet connection and wouldn't have considered this if I had the concern that I may have a data limit.

As a producer, I have maybe streamed bigger shows only a couple of times with my mobile data, but these are always heavily stripped-down shows. Unlimited data has allowed me to 'go live' and do simple streams whilst out on the move which has been useful.

So, what should you get?

The answer to this will rapidly change as mobile service providers continually improve services and give new offers of prices and packages.

The best advice here will be for you to check what service providers are available in your area, and the experiences of other users currently. There's no point going with a company if they don't have good signal where you live.

Generally speaking, you'll want whatever the latest generation of mobile internet is available. At the time of writing, 5G mobile internet is the newest, but 4G is still most common, and 3G is still usable. Judge what you can afford and what you realistically think your needs will be, not just for virtual theatre, but for your internet needs overall.

Remember though, my recommendation is that if you are producing virtual theatre shows, you should go for internet via a router as your first choice and only use mobile data if you have no other option.

A computer or smart device

OK, we've spoken about your internet connection, and established that I think for best results you should aim to stream from a computer, but we will discuss all options anyway. This time starting with smart devices and working up to computers.

Smartphones

The great thing about using your smartphone for virtual theatre is that it's small and therefore very portable, and has a screen, mic and camera all built in.

As discussed in the last section, the ability to use your smartphone to stream from means you are not limited by location, and this can give lots of options for the setting of where you stream from. It means you can stream as you move and can therefore create stories set anywhere using real world locations to great effect.

And because smartphones don't need to be tethered to an internet connection or plugged in (hopefully you'll have it fully charged before your show) you could conceivably do something very cinematic where a performer could concentrate on their acting whilst a crew member follows them as a camera operator. This is something that cannot be achieved from a computer and one of the strengths of using mobile phones to create virtual theatre.

The limitations of smartphones are that their internet connection can be less reliable if you are not in a stable location for signal, and that there are also software limitations compared to PC.

With a small screen where you can't realistically have multiple software running at once, you currently can't create the same level of advanced streams with all the overlays, effects, chat boxes and such like which is possible on your computer.

You will also find that if you need to communicate with text chat during a show, that having to use the same touch screen as you are watching the stream through may be noticeable to audience if you are onscreen. It is much easier to be discreet with a keyboard and mouse on a laptop. Wireless keyboards for your smart device may help with this.

Tablets

For the most part, everything I said about smart phones will apply to streaming from a tablet. Tablets are small enough so they can still be just as portable as a phone, but the larger display has benefits too.

Video conferencing software such as Zoom has limits to how many participants you can see onscreen at one time on a phone, and using a tablet makes more visible without the need to scroll or swipe to see more. If your virtual theatre scene has several people in it at once and you can't see them all, you'll be missing people you may need to react and respond to.

As the gap between the capabilities of tablets and PCs shrink, you can expect that in the future a tablet will be able to handle similar broadcasting software as a PC. For the current time, there aren't huge differences between what can be achieved on a smart phone and tablet devices.

Personal Computers

A desktop or laptop computer will give a virtual theatre producer the most options when creating their shows.

The only disadvantage a computer has over a smart device is that you can't really use them as portably as mentioned with a phone. Even if you were to run a laptop from its battery and tethered it to mobile data, it's just not very practical to use it moving between rooms or out in the streets or in a car as can be achieved with a mobile phone.

A computer, whether desktop or laptop, will allow you to do the most creatively with your show. This is in terms of power, software options and through additional equipment which can elevate a virtual theatre show from looking like a Zoom call, all the way up to shows with a Hollywood style presentation.

What should you get?

Computer specs can be a minefield to understand, as there are several different things to consider that will improve performance. Let's break them down as a starting point, but with new technology continually being developed and released, you'll have to look at what is currently being offered at shops in various price ranges to know what is currently seen as premium or not. Regardless, here are some things to look for to help you judge what computer is right for you.

Processor

The brain of your computer basically. There are multiple companies that produce processors such as AMD and Intel. Look at reviews and a good rule of thumb for components like processors and graphic cards is by looking for ones in computers that people recommend for gaming or video editing.

Higher numbers with tech things will often indicate a more recent or powerful model, such as iPhone 13 being superior to an iPhone 12 etc. It should be noted that this not always the case, and processors can be an example of when this isn't.

For example an Intel i7 processor sounds like it should be better than an Intel i5 processor right? Generally, this may be true, but confusingly instead of every new iteration getting a new number, each numbered processor may get several generations.

So a 5th generation i5 processor may be equal to or in ways better than a 1st generation i7 processor. The advice here would be to find out what year the specific processor released. You can be certain that a 2023 i9 processor will beat out a 2023 i7 processor for example.

Graphics card

Your PC may not need a dedicated graphics card but having one will certainly improve the performance of your video streaming. They are typically most beneficial for people who play graphic intensive video games and video editors. They can be very expensive and will use more energy when installed.

RAM

Much like the processor, you can find different types of RAM and then different generations of each type of RAM. At the time of writing this, many gaming PCs will have 16GB or 32GB of RAM, and it's a case of the more the merrier, which will also help future proof your computer. Although it's usual that you can change or upgrade RAM if needed.

Storage: It's important not to muddle up the amount of RAM with the amount of hard drive. Having a larger hard drive doesn't mean you'll have a better PC than if it had a smaller hard drive. Certainly, if you fill up your hard drive with photos, games and videos you may start to experience that your PC may start to run slower, but the hard drive is just storage.

If you want a hard drive to help improve the performance of your computer you'll want one that has an internal SSD, or Solid State Drive. SSD drives usually have less space and cost more than hard disc drives, but they have much quicker loading times. If you have an SSD and install your operating system (Windows for example) and other important software such as your broadcasting software onto it, they will run faster and smoother than if they were on a hard drive.

It may also be worth getting external hard drives that connect via USB so that you can keep all your games, videos and other documents on there so they won't drag down the performance of your PC. Keeping your PC optimised for the best performance is very important to ensure your virtual theatre shows don't crash or have other technical errors.

Camera

If you plan to do virtual theatre, you'll need a camera so that your audience can see you.

Smart Devices

Every smartphone and tablet will usually come with both front facing and back cameras built into the devices. The back camera is usually the higher quality camera, which is a shame, as you'll need to use the front facing camera so you can monitor both yourself and any other performers on the screen.

The more modern (and usually expensive) the phone, the more capable and impressive the cameras will be.

Here are a couple of ideas for workarounds if you wish to stream from your smart device, but want improved camera results than using the front facing camera. As a warning, both come with extra expense and hassle to set up.

There are adaptors to be able to plug PC webcams into your phone/tablet, and although this may give you a better image than the front facing camera, it does come an at extra expense.

Your best bet if you want to do virtual theatre using your smart device and its rear camera would be to mirror your phone/tablet screen to another monitor or TV. The problem here is that you may not be able to access any onscreen controls you'd need to interact with. A Bluetooth keyboard may overcome this, but again this is extra expense and hassle.

Built in webcam

If you are using a laptop, it's very likely that your laptop has a webcam built in. It's also more likely than not that it's not very good. Now, I don't know this, and you may be perfectly happy with your webcam's results, but unless a really good webcam was a selling point of your laptop, it's probably average at best. The reason for this, is two-fold. Firstly, many people may buy the laptop but never use the webcam, so why make the laptop more expensive than it needs to be with a high-quality webcam that some people will never use? The second reason is because tech companies benefit from being able to sell you additional devices such as webcams and microphones, so why give you the best already built into your laptop?

Either way, the built-in webcam on a laptop will probably be serviceable, but not much beyond if you hope to deliver the best quality image to your audience.

USB Webcam

This is the route I'd recommend whether you have a built-in webcam or not. A wired USB webcam has the advantage of being able to be repositioned to somewhere most useful for you. This may be directly above your monitor, or somewhere slightly away from your computer if there is better light or noise you wish to be a little further back from.

You could also have multiple webcams plugged into your PC and use your video meeting software or the other broadcasting software to change camera angles. This could be particularly useful if you wish to go from a close up of your face to a shot of your full body.

I'd suggest you get a camera capable to shoot a minimum of Full HD at 1080p resolution. For a lower quality option, you could go for one that is an HD camera at 720p, although I wouldn't recommend anything lower resolution than this.

If you have a powerful computer and fast internet connection you could consider a 4K resolution camera, but keep in mind that unless you stream in 4K, and your audience have 4K capable displays they won't see it in this resolution.

The camera I currently use is a Logitech Streamcam, and is a Full HD camera which gives a clear image, and has the benefit of being able to be mounted to record in either landscape or portrait orientation.

DSLR Camera connected via HDMI

The final option we'll cover for now is the option to use a camera that you would normally use for still photography and videography as a webcam. If you have a DSLR or Mirrorless camera from the likes of Canon, Nikon, Panasonic etc, it's possible to connect these to your computer to use as a webcam.

This is by far the most expensive option, as not only will you need the camera itself, which can easily run into hundreds of pounds, but you'll need extra equipment to use the camera with your computer.

To do this you'll need a video capture card such as the Elgato Cam Link which plugs into the computer and then allows you to connect your camera with a micro-HDMI to HDMI cable. You'll almost certainly also need a power cable for your camera to give it continuous power.

After this, you'll have the option to get multiple lenses that can offer the ability to zoom in or have varying levels of clarity.

Microphone

Some would argue that good quality audio is more important than good quality video, and I can certainly understand why. If your image is lower resolution, or poorly framed, audiences are much more likely to be forgiving than if you have poor audio that they can't hear well. People listen to podcasts and the radio all the time where they can hear but not see what is going on. How often do people still watch silent movies?

Before you read on

When investing in a microphone, I would suggest you consider if you have other potential uses for a microphone? If you're interested in voice over acting, podcasting, internet radio or filmmaking, you could consider getting a higher quality mic for multiple purposes as well as virtual theatre. This will help justify any costs and you'll get more bang for your buck!

Smart Devices

Much like with the cameras, phones and tablets have microphones built in, and usually the quality of the mics are fairly reasonable. After all, a smartphone wouldn't be very smart if it didn't function well as a phone and people couldn't hear each other well on calls.

Regardless, you can find a variety of microphones for smartphones, as many people use their phones to record interviews or podcasts. Lavalier mics that clip on to your shirt can be relatively cheap and can boost your audio quality.

Built-in computer mics

Just as many laptops have cameras built-in, they usually have a microphone built in. This will do the trick for your most basic needs, but as we'll cover in a later section, you may find that you benefit from a second mic even if you do put a built-in mic to work. This is because you may want a separate second mic to ensure both the audience and other performers can hear you.

USB mics

There are many high-quality USB mics from companies such as Rode, Blue, Elgato and Razer. Research what current popular mics are for podcasters, and this will inform you of some makes and models to look at. You may find that a popular company produces a cheaper mic if budget is a concern.

XLR Mics

You'll often find that high quality mics made for radio or film usage connect via an XLR cable connection. A popular mic which I often use is the Rode Procaster, and this is an XLR mic. To use these on your computer you'll need a minimum of an XLR to USB adaptor, but you may also find that you need an in between device to supply power to the microphone.

There are many USB audio mixers available such as those from Behringer which allow you to plug in your mic and feature many dials and sliders to adjust your audio.

Field Recorders

Field recorders such as the Zoom H4n, H5 and H6 are great for recording audio for film shoots and for podcasts and radio. They feature a high-quality mic built in, and can also have a variety of types of microphones plugged into them, such as the above discussed XLR mics. They can be plugged into your computer with a USB cable and provide great audio.

Additional accessories for microphones

Whichever type of mic you go for, you may find that you can improve your results with an extra accessory or two for the clearest audio.

Pop Shield

A pop shield is the dark circular disc you may have seen in front of microphones when people talk on the radio or at recording studios. Whenever we say words with the letters P, T and K in, people give out a puff of air and this can result in an unpleasant scratchy sound going into the mic. A pop shield stops this puff of air getting through.

Sound absorption foam

Another thing you may have seen in recording studios is that the walls are usually covered in bumpy foam panels. This is to soundproof the room to ensure that outside noise doesn't get picked up on the recordings. This may feel overkill for your virtual theatre shows but depending how much you want to invest into it, or if you have other uses of your mic, this could level up your game significantly.

If you're not ready to go all in on fixing foam to your walls, you could get a microphone isolation shield which is a like an open box or a folding shield that has foam panels and your mic sits inside.

Mic stands, scissor arms and shock mounts

You'll be amazed just how much a high-quality mic can pick up every sound. This goes from every accidental tap of the mic through to anything that disturbs what the mic is stood on. To limit hearing any unwanted movements you should consider what you use to hold your microphone.

Many mics come with tabletop stands and these may be fine for your purposes, but you could consider getting a scissor arm that will clamp to your computer desk, or allow you to hang your mic just over head.

A good shock mount will also mean that if you do knock the mic stand that you don't hear any loud bangs or rattles as the shock mount will absorb the impact and prevent extra sounds getting through.

What Mics I have used

I currently use an Elgato Wave 3 as my main computer mic, but also have a Rode Procaster. I have also found using my Zoom H6 field recorder plugged in via USB to be an effective high-quality mic.

Lighting

Even if you have a good camera, you may not get good results if you don't have good lighting. If you're making a show, you will want to be in control of the lighting just as you are in control of your performance.

Natural light

Being near a window to use natural light is one option, but with changing weather and seasons you can't really know what lighting you'll get from one day to the next. You may also want to be careful if you have a window visible in your shot or next to you as the light coming through could cause you to appear backlit, or over exposed if too much light is pouring in on you.

Room light

You could always just switch on the electric light on your ceiling, or even use a common desk lamp. Doing this, you may find results you are happy with, if your goal is just to be suitably lit and seen by the audience. This can lack a professional look, as room light is room light and will look just like someone in their room.

Ring lights

A very popular and often quite cheap option is to get a ring light. These will usually come with a mount so that you can attach your webcam or smart phone within a ring of light, and this will evenly light your face as you look towards your camera.

They are usually adjustable in their brightness and tone and are very popular with people who create videos for TikTok and Instagram.

LED panels

In the olden days film lights would be large, bright and burn very hot. I once literally burned three lines into my fingertips on a film shoot by picking up a light that hadn't sufficiently cooled down!

Nowadays these old lights are mostly replaced by LED panels which are much safer and arguably produce better results. They are quite compact, and you can usually adjust the brightness and temperature, and sometimes even adjust the colour.

I would recommend you have a minimum of two light panels, or three if you are using a green screen to add virtual backgrounds. If you have just one light, you'll want to find the best positioning of it which will probably be somewhere just behind the camera. This will give you the most even lighting on your face when looking towards the camera.

If you have just one light and it is to one side of you, the other side of your face will appear more shadowy. If this is an effect you want for your show then you can do it this way, but I'd still say to have at least two lights with one being either side of you. And when I say either side of you, I don't mean directly to your left and right.

Imagine you are stood in the middle of an analogue clock which is laid out flat. Now if we imagine that your camera is placed at the 12 position, you'll want your lights positioned at the 10 and 2 positions.

If you are using a greenscreen, you may also benefit from having another light to evenly light the greenscreen behind you. This way you won't cast shadows onto the greenscreen from the other lights and the green will stay a solid colour and work to the best effect.

What I use

I currently use five lights, although rarely all at the same time. I have two LED panels made by Aputure which I have had for a few years for film shoots I have worked on. They have adjustable brightness levels, and you can swap out plastic colour panels to change the temperature effect.

I also have a ring light which I primarily use to light a second, overhead camera when filming onto a desk to show objects in my hands.

Finally, my main current lights are two Elgato Air lights. I can control these via either an app or from my Stream Deck (which I'll cover shortly) You can easily adjust the brightness and warmth of the light, but for me, the main benefit to my endeavours with virtual theatre is that I could control them remotely without having to physically go over to them and adjust them.

Multiple monitors

This may not be essential if you're just performing in virtual theatre shows, but if you're the technician/producing virtual shows, I would say having multiple screens is essential.

I usually use a minimum of three screens, which not only feels cool, like I'm running a television studio, but also makes life a lot easier.

To use my current set up as the example, this is how I would have each of my screens set up.

Screen 1:

On this screen I will have the video meeting such as Zoom so that I can see everyone, and also access any controls for spotlighting participants, muting them and such like.

Screen 2:

Will be my broadcasting software such as OBS or SLOBS. This is where I'll monitor and control any onscreen graphics and effects.

Screen 3:

Will be where I monitor and interact with audience chat messages. I'll also have at least one internet browser tab open to monitor the stream to make sure we're still broadcasting and check how bad any time delay appears to be from an audience perspective.

These are the three screens I currently use, and if I need anything additional open, I'll usually have other windows or programs open underneath what I've outlined above.

However...I do sometimes use a forth screen, and in an ideal world I'd be happy to have five or six. If I had a monitor for everything I may need, I would have the following:

Screen 4:

I sometimes use a custom piece of software I developed as a scoreboard for certain shows, and when using it I usually have it sit beneath my chat messages on screen 3. If I could have it on its own screen it would make life easier.

Screen 5:

I may sometimes need to access a website or word document to discuss on a review or panel show. I usually find that I open this over the top of my Zoom meeting which isn't ideal as it means I can't always see the reactions of the other performers on the show. Having this on an additional monitor would enable me to see both easier.

Screen 6:

Other software. Depending, what your show is, there may be a need for another piece of software to be open, such as an art programme, a video game, or a Dungeons and Dragons app to roll dice and display maps etc. A sixth screen would enable this to be always accessed.

So even though I only regularly use three screens, you can see how the needs of more complex shows may benefit from more screen real estate.

I'm certain that for most people, unless they start adding bells and whistles to make their shows more complex, they would be able to comfortably cope with just one screen.

Just as a further note on your monitors, you have many choices when it comes to monitors. Curved screens provide better viewing angles and ultrawide screen monitors may mean you can have multiple programs open on just the one screen.

Some people orientate one screen to a portrait position as this may allow for more apps to be open at once. Also, a 4K or 8K screen at a larger size will also allow you to have more programs running on a single screen as well.

Other equipment to consider

Smart devices

All of what I've just said about multiple screens doesn't really apply to smart devices. Some tablets allow you to go into split screen mode and you could have two apps open at once, but in my experience, this would just stop you seeing full screen on your video meeting and cause more issues.

If you have them, you can use multiple smart devices to achieve the same as having a multi-screen computer setup. For example, if you had a tablet and you were running Zoom on it, you could then also have your phone out to monitor the chat on YouTube.

Of course, you could also do this if you were running your shows on a computer, and only had one monitor. A smart phone near by could mean you don't have to have extra tabs open, and this would also mean there would be less drag on the computer's resources.

Greenscreen

Depending on your show, you may decide to use virtual backgrounds. Software such as Zoom and Microsoft Teams will allow you to digitally remove your background and replace it with an image or video.

If you don't have a green screen, the software will detect your movement and what it identifies as a person and remove the background. This is never as clean a removal as when using a green screen. If you do virtual backgrounds without a greenscreen, you'll get much better results if you have good lighting.

If you have a green screen, the software will be able to detect just the single green colour and remove it, which gives a much cleaner effect to cut people out from their background. Again, good lighting is key for best results.

It is worth noting that you don't have to have a 'green' screen. You can usually set the software to remove whichever colour you want, but the reason why we use the colour green most frequently, is because it doesn't commonly conflict with people's hair, skin, or eye colour. Also, people don't generally wear the standard greenscreen shade of green very often on their clothes.

Stream Deck

A Stream Deck is a specific device, created by Elgato, but it's also become the common name for the type of device it is. A Stream Deck is a customisable keypad. Alternatives include the Razer Tartarus Keypad, and the Loupedeck.

What it allows you to do is assign its buttons to specific actions as short cuts and hot keys. The Stream Deck comes either with 6, 15 or 32 buttons, and behind each button is a screen which you can customise with text and graphics.

You can create folders which you can assign to a button which in theory means that by having folders within folders you could have an infinite amount of buttons set up for different software.

I have folders assigned to buttons for each of the Extreme Improv XStreamed shows we do online. Each folder contains buttons for onscreen graphics, music, scene changes etc that I need to run the shows.

Being able to access all the tools I need from the Stream Deck means I don't have to scroll through onscreen menus or go from programme to programme as it's all there in one place.

I can also control my lights from the Stream Deck and have folders set up with short cuts for Word, Photoshop and more.

I can't put over enough how useful this device is and how much it streamlines producing virtual theatre.

Elgato also offer a mobile app version of the Steam Deck which works via a subscription service. Functionally it turns your mobile device into a touch screen version of a Stream Deck, but some won't like the lack of tactile buttons with this solution.

Autocue

If the show you are making is scripted, you could add an autocue to your setup. Having an autocue, or teleprompter as it is also known, will allow you to easily read dialogue for plays, video podcasts and explainer videos whilst being able to look directly into the camera.

An autocue is a kind of camera mount which you attach your camera to. The camera then sits behind an angled piece of glass with a dark hood over it. In front of the angled glass is a platform where you can place a screen such as a tablet or smartphone.

Then using autocue apps, you paste in your text which can either be set to auto play or be controlled by the user. Bluetooth devices such as a specific teleprompter controller, or generic keyboard or game controllers work just fine.

The text on the smart device will be displayed as a mirror image and will usually display as white text on a black background. When placed on the autocue in front of the angled glass you will be able to read off the text which will be reflected the correct way to read, and will enable your eyeline to be directly into the lens of the camera.

A USB Hub

A USB hub will allow you to plug in additional USB devices into your computer. You may or may not need this, but if you go for an advanced setup, you may find you are quickly running out of USB ports.

In summary

In chapter 12 I'll go over exactly what equipment I use at the time of writing, but for now, go through everything here and decide what is essential and what fits your budget. You can get started as long as you have a computer or smart device, and the sky is the limit for how many bells and whistles you want to add to build the dream setup.

9: SOFTWARE AND SERVICES

Now let's take a look at the software or online services you'll need, and what role it will play in creating your virtual theatre show. To create and broadcast a show, there are three categories of software we'll be looking at:

Video Meeting/Conferencing Software: This will allow any cast members to see and hear each other in a virtual meeting space.

Broadcasting Software: Software designed to live stream your show out to the internet to various platforms. These will usually offer a way for the person streaming to add their webcam, but do not natively include a way to connect various people from other locations.

Combined Video Meeting and Broadcasting Software: Software that will allow people to connect to each other for video calls, and also has the capacity to broadcast to social media platforms without requiring separate broadcasting software.

Video Meeting/Conferencing Software and Combined Video Meeting/Broadcasting Software

The most important piece of software you'll need is a way to connect your team together via video.

There are continually new pieces of software entering the market, and the features of these will continue to be updated many times in the future. So once again, if you're reading this many years after the publication date, there may be new software on the market, but the important thing is that you have video conferencing software to use.

Things like Skype and Face Time have been ways to have video calls for years, and Skype has long been a useful way to connect people for video podcasts. It was during the COVID-19 pandemic that Zoom became the market leader in video meeting software, and it wouldn't take long before people started using it for purposes beyond just work or social calls, such as virtual theatre.

This is important to note, as although the performing arts community have adopted using these types of software for creating shows, they were not designed for it. Over time new features have been added to these software which make them more useful for virtual theatre, and this will continue in the future. Until a large-scale piece of software is released that is designed primarily around virtual theatre, you'll should expect to use workarounds to achieve everything you could want.

Currently, Zoom is the biggest of the video conferencing software giants. It's the main one I use, and it's the most used video meeting software in the world. In terms of familiarity, it's very likely that most of your performers and crew will have used it at some point and know the basics of how to use it.

Here is a list of video conferencing software or online services options:

Dedicated Video Meeting Software

- Microsoft Teams
- Skype
- Google Meet
- Facebook Messenger Rooms

Combined Video Meeting and Broadcasting Software

- Zoom
- StreamYard
- Restream
- Discord

Additionally, the following social media platforms also offer the ability to connect a video call with others and stream live directly on the platform. These all have restrictions such as number of participants whom can take part, and limited design options as we will discuss later. Other social platforms may offer an individual the ability to go live, but not offer native ways for multiple people to connect via video.

- Facebook
- Instagram
- TikTok

Features You'll Want

I currently use Zoom as my go to piece of software to connect my performers, but as software develops, you may want to explore any current software to see if it has the features you need. Here are what I consider as the essential features I'd need from video meeting software to create a successful virtual theatre show.

Number of participants

Extreme Improv Xstreamed virtual shows can typically feature between 5-12 performers at a time, and it is usual that we limit any scenes to a maximum of 5 people at once. Having more can just become unmanageable, as the cast struggle to avoid speaking over each other, and for the audience to be able to see everyone and follow who is speaking.

If your show demands a much larger cast, then many of the software mentioned will allow dozens if not hundreds of people all in the same meeting, although there are frequently limits to how many can be displayed on screen at any one time.

Being able to have many participants in the video call meeting is also useful as a way to have an audience as part of the meeting with you.

Some of the software mentioned has limits to the number of participants you can have in a meeting, or to the length of the meeting you can have if there are above a certain number of participants at one time. If there are limits, you can usually pay a monthly fee to lift these restrictions, so play around with the software and see which one fits your needs first, before paying out money.

Spotlight participants

Say you're doing a virtual performance of Romeo and Juliet, and you have a cast of 12 people. You'll want to use software that allows you to put the focus on just the actors playing Romeo and Juliet, otherwise the romantic scenes will just feel awkward if there are 10 third wheels also on screen!

Some of the software will simply allow you to spotlight a single 'speaker', or the software may detect who is currently talking and automatically change the screen to feature that person for everyone else. Ideally, you'll want host controls so that your director or technician can spotlight multiple characters at a time, and only the ones who are relevant to the scene.

Virtual backgrounds

Virtual backgrounds allow you to remove the view of the actual environment and replace it with a custom image or video. These can be useful if they are designed to reflect the location, or tone of your show.

Change meeting background

The participants in your video meeting will usually appear in a rectangular box that shows what their webcam is picking up. Depending how many people are in the meeting, you may also see empty black space filling the gaps around the performer's individual webcam view.

Being able to change the black background to a custom image or video of your choosing can distinguish your show from others. It can also help give the feeling that people are watching a show where effort has been put into the design, and not just watching some people on a video call.

Add your branding

As well as being able to change the background behind the view of performers webcams, you may want to add a logo, or other branding of your show/theatre company which can display in one corner or the side of the screen.

On screen chat

Some of the mentioned software/online services natively incorporate the ability to display online chat messages that have come from your audience. For some types of show you may not want this, or find this a distraction, but for interactive shows, or if you're working on building a community, you may want to display the chat on screen to show off your audience engagement. This will also make it easy for YouTube viewers to see what viewers on Facebook are saying and vice versa.

Private chat with your team

Sometimes during a show, a member of you cast/crew may need to relay a message to another cast member. This may be to highlight a technical difficulty, or it may be to check in on a performer, or to coordinate something for the performance.

Unfortunately, a drawback of virtual theatre is you can't whisper backstage or take five minutes in the dressing room like you may with a live show. Chat functions that aren't displayed to the audience are useful in this regard and can improve the slickness of a show.

10: BROADCASTING SOFTWARE

If you want to broadcast yourself onto social media platforms, you can either do it directly from some of the platforms (we'll cover this momentarily), but if you want to customise your show, you will need some broadcasting software. Here we'll look at some options that are currently available.

Going live directly from YouTube, Facebook etc.

Most social media platforms will offer a way for their users to 'go live' and stream from their computers or smart devices. Doing so can be as easy as a few clicks to set up a stream, name it, and allow access to your webcam.

When you start setting up a stream it may give you the option to immediately go live, or it may ask if you'd like to stream via broadcasting software such as those we'll cover shortly. If you choose to broadcast via broadcasting software, the social media platform will provide you with a 'stream key'. A stream key is a unique code that when used on broadcasting software will link your stream to your social media channel and allow access to stream the video.

Combined video meeting and broadcasting software

The following software can all connect people together in a virtual space, and broadcast to one or more social media platforms without the need of additional broadcasting software. You may find the simplicity of using one application preferable, and what they offer may meet your needs from a design or function perspective. If you want to add more function or customise the look and feel of your shows, I suggest using a video meeting software in conjunction with dedicated broadcasting software, as these will offer more options to tweak the look and feel of your broadcasts.

Zoom

It's possible to go live directly from Zoom, and whilst its features are continually improving, it is a video calling and work meeting based software and wasn't designed for streamers and virtual theatre. Therefore, it lacks many features of other broadcasting software on this list at the time of writing.

This said, the Zoom developers are continually adding features which give virtual theatre producers more design and function options to work with. It is also extremely widely used and if used in conjunction with broadcasting software, it is excellent to use for handling the video meeting needs of a virtual theatre show.

StreamYard

StreamYard works directly from your internet browser without the need to download additional applications. It combines the functions of video call software with broadcasting software to be an all-in-one kind of package. There is a subscription cost to using the fuller versions of StreamYard, but there is also a free option with reduced features. Some will really like the features and presentation of StreamYard, but even the fullest version doesn't offer as much customisation as you can create in dedicated broadcasting software.

Restream Studio

Restream Studio is very similar to Streamyard, and is another browser based video meeting software which allows you to customise the look of your show, and broadcast out to several platforms at once.

Additionally, Restream offer the service to stream to multiple platforms via other broadcasting software like OBS and SLOBS.

Discord

Discord is an all-in-one communication platform and allows users to host video and voice calls, and has chat and forum like discussion features. It is possible to broadcast shows to other Discord users, but it doesn't allow you to natively broadcast these streams to other social platforms.

If you want to use Discord to host your video meeting, design your show and stream to the likes of YouTube or Facebook, you would also need to use another piece of software to screen capture the Discord stream.

Dedicated broadcasting software

The following software will allow you to create broadcasts that will stream out to one or more social media platforms at a time.

They do not feature built in video meeting functionality, but all will allow the person streaming to add in their webcam and mic, which makes them great for producing solo theatre shows, podcasts and reviews. You can use any of them to screen capture the video feed from video meeting software such as Zoom or Skype, and have many ways to customise the design of your show with graphics, videos and overlays. My recommendation is to use dedicated broadcasting software to design your show and add in the video feed from a dedicated or hybrid video meeting software to get the best of both worlds.

OBS (Open Broadcaster Software)

OBS is the most commonly used broadcasting software out there. It's open source which means that anyone can create plugins and improvements for it, and as such there are tons of things you can do with OBS to add to your stream. Another benefit of loads of people using it means that there are literally thousands of tutorials available which will teach you how to do everything and anything you could imagine.

SLOBS (Stream Labs Open Broadcaster Software)

Stream Labs have created a version of OBS on top of the open source OBS which adds unique features to their platform. Function wise, the two are very similar, and the internet will continue to debate which is superior.

XSplit Broadcaster

XSplit is similar to the likes of OBS, SLOBS and Twitch Studio, and is designed with lots of useful features and a clear user interface. It allows you to connect directly to many social media platforms to broadcast to, and therefore doesn't require using stream keys to set up.

There is a free version of XSplit Broadcaster, but certain features are locked behind a paywall.

Twitch Studio

Twitch Studio is functionality wise is very similar to others such as OBS or XSplit. Created by the team at Twitch, it is designed to be an entry level to mid-level broadcasting software. It's not as feature rich as some on this list, but it offers a decent amount of customisation options, and it has a layout that makes everything logical and easy to understand.

I'll mention this wherever I discuss Twitch Studio, but it's important to note that Twitch Studio will only stream to the Twitch platform and cannot stream to the likes of Facebook or YouTube at the time of writing.

Mobile Streaming Apps

The following are smart device apps which will allow you to stream from a mobile phone or tablet. Whilst not as feature rich as computer-based broadcasting software, they work in a similar way where you can add design elements, broadcast directly from your device's camera, or screen capture more advanced video meetings.

Omlet Arcade – Mobile

Omlet Arcade is a smart device app which allows you to broadcast a screenshare of your mobile phone or tablet to one or more social media accounts. This can be useful for streaming video conference meetings to multiple platforms at once from your smart device, or for streaming podcast, tutorial or gaming content with commentary.

The app does allow you to stream directly from your device's camera. This could be particularly useful for multi-streaming stage performances.

Stream Labs Mobile App

The Stream Labs mobile app offers advanced design tools to create live streams from a smart device. This includes the ability to add themes, overlays, text, and widgets.

It also allows you to screen capture any apps you have running such as video meetings, or go live using the camera built into your device.

Whilst it allows you to add several design elements, it is still a long way off doing all you can do on the computer version of Stream Labs OBS.

11: OTHER USEFUL SOFTWARE

If you want to add cool graphics, logos, and video elements to your stream, you could either source these elements from places on the web, or you could make them yourself.

Designing graphics and video editing may not be your area of expertise, or you may not have the time or interest to make these yourself, and if so, that's fine. The internet is filled with thousands or millions of free or cheap graphics and videos for use in projects. Look up public domain or royalty free images to see what is available. You could also consider hiring an artist to produce custom logos or overlays for your stream.

Personally, I like to be hands on and design or customise on screen elements where I can. As such I find the following software very useful when designing a virtual theatre show.

Art programmes

Adobe Photoshop

Photoshop is the most well-known computer art programme in the world. Whether you have a standalone copy, or are subscribed to Adobe Creative Cloud to access several of the Adobe programmes, there is a huge amount you can do to create beautiful stream elements.

GIMP

GIMP (GNU Image Manipulation Program) is a free open-source alternative to Photoshop which has a huge number of features.

Procreate

If you are an iPad user, I'd also highly recommend the app called Procreate. As an alternative to Photoshop which you can use on the go, I've found it very useful to keep designing art assets when away from my home computer.

Video Editing software

When designing your virtual theatre shows, you may want to use animated elements such as video virtual backgrounds or pop up graphics or title cards that are more than static images. Whether you film things, create 2D or 3D animations yourself, or source royalty free footage, having video elements can certainly add to the atmosphere or sense of fun of your show.

At the most basic level, using a video editor will allow you to cut the length of videos and render them in stream friendly formats. If you have clips at high resolutions, it will put more strain on your computer and internet connection. If these elements are only in the background or displayed as small or infrequently, you won't need to have these at full quality.

In terms of which software to use here are a few options to explore:

- Adobe Premiere Pro
- DaVinci Resolve
- Magix Vegas Pro
- Hitfilm
- PowerDirector 365
- Final Cut Pro
- Adobe Premiere Elements
- Apple iMovie

Deciding which video editing software is best for you will depend on a huge number of factors such as cost, platform, learning curve, features and whether they are pay once or subscription based.

What I use

My main video editing software is Magix Vegas Pro which I favoured due to it being a software you can buy once and don't have to subscribe to, although subscription-based versions have been introduced in recent years. I also found many positive reviews of like its ease of use. Whilst there are a huge number of features to learn, it is for the most part a straightforward piece of software to use.

I do also use Hitfilm for some visual effects which I can't achieve in Vegas, and although I don't regularly use it, I am happy to use Apple iMovie on my iPad if I want to create short videos or promo materials when I can't access my PC.

12: THE SOFTWARE AND HARDWARE I USE TO CREATE VIRTUAL THEATRE SHOWS

I get it. You've read through all the options I've laid out for what computer, software and accessories to get, but you may not want to have to weigh up all the options. You just want to know an option that works. Understandable.

I'll now go over what I use to create virtual theatre shows at the time of writing this book. As a heads up, it will get outdated pretty quickly, and I want you to keep in mind that if I don't use something in particular, it doesn't mean it is not good. Something might be better than what I currently use, and I may just continue to use it because I'm used to it and haven't had a chance to swap things over yet.

I'll also say that whilst I find that I can create elaborate virtual theatre shows, I am far from having the dream setup. I have budget and space limitations the same as the next fellow. Much of what I use, I have assembled over many years and most of it is second hand or were things I got on sale, so don't feel you need to rush to get everything all at once. As long as you have a laptop with a webcam, or smart device, you will be able to get started making virtual theatre shows.

What I use will evolve, but any limits or compromises I have made on my setup just further prove that you don't need the ultimate setup to get going and make your virtual theatre dreams come true!

Hardware

Computer

I stream from a MSI Gaming Laptop with an i7 processor, built in SSD and 32GB Ram.

Monitors

I use a 3-monitor setup. I would suggest most people should have at least two if you want to be able to create elaborate virtual theatre shows. One monitor is the built-in laptop monitor. Another is a Wacom Cintiq, which is an interactive pen display, so you can use a special pen to draw on the screen. My third monitor is a small HD television. Yup – not even an actual monitor. I'd love to have additional ultra widescreen 8K curved monitors and vertical monitors mounted to the side, but I'm perfectly capable of making my shows with the three I have.

Wired internet with an Ethernet Cable

I plug my computer into the internet with an ethernet cable for a better connection than Wi-Fi. I just have the standard router that the internet company provided, and the cable is just a generic one from Amazon.

Keyboard and mouse

I use both an Amazon branded rollerball mouse and a Trust vertical mouse, but that's because I get back pain and changing the way I use a mouse helped. I also use a generic cheap wired keyboard in addition to the laptop keyboard, again so it helps with back pain...but it's just a cheap one so I won't recommend a specific brand.

USB Hub

I have a wall socket powered USB hub so that I can plug in my additional monitors, mouse, keyboard, external hard drives etc etc.

Stream Deck

I use an Elgato Stream Deck as an additional keypad that I can assign hotkeys to. It is just about the most useful accessory I have as I can pretty much run an entire virtual theatre show from it. You'll notice I use a few Elgato branded accessories, and this is partly because they are easy to control via the Stream Deck.

Webcam

I use a Logitech Streamcam. I do also use an Elgato Cam Link with a Panasonic G7, but use this less regularly now I have the Streamcam.

Microphone

I use an Elgato Wave 3 USB mic. I also use the mic built into my Streamcam and previously used to plug in my Zoom H5 field recorder to use as a mic as well.

Greenscreen

I hang a greenscreen cloth behind my computer chair. It's a cheap one, but if well lit it works perfectly. Some people use those pop-up ones, and whilst I have one, I find it a pain to fold down.

Lights

I use two Elgato Key Light Air lights for lighting me/my greenscreen. I also have a generic cheap ring light, and an older Aputure LED light panel that I use on occasion.

iPad Pro

If I can't do shows from my computer setup, I usually just do them from my trusty old iPad Pro. Creating shows from a smart device means the shows I create on it are limited in many ways compared to PC, but I can get the job done.

Software

Please note that all the software featured in this book will continue to get updates, so if I don't use or recommend something now, it doesn't mean you shouldn't ever use it. Far from it.

One of the reasons I feature guides for many different software is because I understand that people will have their preferences based on many factors. This may be simplicity to use, familiarity, cost, user interface, brand loyalty or a range of other factors. For me though, here is what I use.

Zoom

I use Zoom to handle the video meeting aspect of creating my shows. Unless I am streaming from my iPad, I won't stream directly from Zoom, and will use additional broadcasting software in conjunction with Zoom. For me it is the most feature rich video meeting software at the time of writing.

Restream and StreamYard

I use restream to multi-stream my shows to various social media platforms at the same time. I also sometimes use Restream Studio for some shows, as whilst Zoom is my primary video meeting software, I like the different look and feel that Restream Studio offers.

I mention StreamYard as in my experience, it seems nearly identical to Restream Studio, so can recommend it equally.

Stream Labs OBS

My primary Broadcasting software choice is Stream Labs OBS. I like the interface, and all the customisation you can do to the streams you create. It is nearly identical to OBS in most ways, and I swapped from using OBS to SLOBS a while ago and have just kept going with it.

OBS

I do sometimes still use OBS, and at some point, may fully return to OBS, but as I said, in my experience OBS and SLOBS feel nearly identical to use. OBS will certainly have more user created plugins and SLOBS will have the Stream Labs specific themes etc.

I would note that Twitch Studio seemed very similar, but I didn't like the limitation of only streaming to Twitch. I also really liked using XSplit, so whilst I may explore that more in the future, I don't currently us it as my primary broadcasting software.

13: DESIGNING THE LOOK OF YOUR SHOW

Let's look at how you can customise the look and functionality of your virtual theatre show. In this section we'll go through several popular software and give ideas and guides of how to design your show.

As a warning, which I've said before, but will say again, everything I've written here is correct at the time of writing. A lot of what I've written should still be a useful method for the foreseeable future as the ideas of what you'll need are unlikely to change. But as this section is more of a step-by-step style guide, things may change if the developers of the software listed update their programmes.

So, if something says, 'the tool is on the panel on the left' and now it's on the right, the important thing to look for is the name of the tool.

I would also recommend that you take a look at the guides for each piece of software, even if you only plan to use one or two of them. This way, you'll be able to learn a little about what each programme can offer compared to the others, and you may get ideas of things to try in your chosen software.

I: DESIGNING YOUR SHOW ON ZOOM

Before we begin

This guide is based around the functions that are available in the most basic free version of Zoom, and/or its lowest cost paid Pro tier. There are Business and Enterprise price tiers, and other options such as Zoom Webinar which have much higher costs attached to them. These also allow for extra functions such as a high number of concurrent meeting participants and the ability to add branding, but for the purposes of creating most virtual theatre performances, these won't be needed.

Getting started

In this guide for Zoom, we'll cover all the tools and design options that are available to create your show in Zoom itself. In later sections, we'll then take what we have created here in Zoom and add the Zoom meeting into other broadcasting software such as OBS.

In these later sections I will cover these other broadcasting software options and may refer back to things you need to do in Zoom in conjunction with them.

It is easier with a friend

If you are designing a show with a video conferencing software, I would always suggest having a minimum of two participants in the video meeting whilst designing. This is because a meeting with just one participant will show that participant filling the whole screen and you won't get a sense of the layout of when there are multiple people onscreen. Certain tools or functions may also not be available if there is only one person in the meeting.

The good news is that you don't actually need another person to join the meeting if you don't have someone available to ask. If you can do so, it is easy to join the meeting a second time yourself using both a computer and a smart device.

Virtual backgrounds

Each user of Zoom will have the option to change the background of their webcam view to what is known as a virtual background. This means you can replace the view of your room or greenscreen with an image or video.

This can be great for sharing branding, or for adding a background that gives a sense of location/atmosphere for your virtual theatre show.

Virtual backgrounds have to be set up by the individual users, and cannot be controlled by the meeting host. Keep this in mind if you are the designer for the show, as you may have to provide everyone with the relevant images/videos in advance and guide them how to change their backgrounds.

Here's how to change your virtual background

Changing virtual backgrounds on a computer

Next to the control to Stop/Start video there is a little arrow that looks like this ^. Click it and you'll see that it says 'Choose virtual background...'. This will bring up the settings menu to the backgrounds and effects tab.

Here you can choose between having no virtual background, blurring the background behind you, using one of Zoom's included images or videos, or adding your own. Once you've added your own, these will appear here to select, and you won't have to upload your own every time.

To add your own, click the + (plus) symbol and choose to add either an image or video.

As a note, it is important not to add a huge file. A lower resolution photo, or short video clip is all that is needed. Videos will play on loop and do not play any sound.

Once you've selected your video, you'll also notice you can tick to say 'I have a greenscreen'. If you are using a greenscreen behind yourself, I would suggest to have this box checked as it will produce a much cleaner greenscreen effect. Depending on your lighting, you may experience that the greenscreen effect works better with good lighting, or that things start to look glitchy in poor lighting.

If you have a different coloured backdrop, you'll see that you can change the colour of your greenscreen if you have the box checked and this will bring up a target sight to choose any colour from your environment. You don't literally have to have a green 'greenscreen'.

And as a final note, if you wear green, you will start to disappear, so make sure whatever you're wearing doesn't match your greenscreen colour.

Changing virtual backgrounds on a smart device

On your smart device, open up the three-dot menu and choose Backgrounds and Effects.

Here you will be able to add or choose an image to be your virtual background. Unlike on a computer, you cannot currently add a video.

You can select to use a greenscreen if you have one. As a note though, if you are likely to use your smart device for virtual theatre from a variety of locations, be aware that it is easy to leave 'I have a greenscreen' switched on. If you are then joining a Zoom meeting from where you don't have a greenscreen, this may need switching off again as the greenscreen effect won't work properly.

Video Filters

Also available from the backgrounds and effects tab of the settings menu are video filters. These are a mix of camera filters, overlays and face filters that will appear within each participant's webcam view.

The camera filters will allow you to change the tone of the whole image, such as adjusting the brightness, contrast or putting the webcam into black and white mode. The use of the black and white filter in particular is useful as a way to give a visual indicator of a flashback, or if a character is dead, or eliminated from a competition.

The overlays may add things like borders or images around your webcam view.

Face filters are similar to the filters available in Snapchat and add virtual masks and costume elements to a person and track their movement.

Avatars

This is a new feature at the time of writing and allows a participant to replace themselves with a digital avatar which is tracked to move in sync with their movements. This includes head, and mouth movements and can even mimic facial expressions, blink and know when you stick your tongue out.

At the time of writing, it doesn't track arm or hand gestures or movements, but this is a feature I expect will greatly evolve and update many times in the coming years.

Immersive view

Immersive view allows you to change the background on Zoom to make it appear as if the participants are together in the same room. You can replace the background of the meeting with images of rooms such as classrooms or kitchens or use any of your own images to create virtual sets. It also allows you to alter the position and size of participants on screen.

To go into immersive view mode, click on the view settings and choose immersive view. A menu will pop up and you can either add your own image or use one of the provided ones.

If you use a provided view, the participants will be placed into pre-defined locations on the screen, and you will be limited to how much you can move and resize the view of each person. If you want to change their positions on screen, just drag and drop the person onto a different area of the screen.

If you use your own backdrop, you will be able to drag and drop people onto any position on screen. This includes that you can have participants overlap each other. This is a very useful thing for your cast to play around with as they can give the sense of interacting with each other physically.

You can also resize participants to give a sense of people being in the foreground or background of a location. Keep in mind that you will still be limited to how much of the participant can be seen on their webcam view.

So, for example, if you want a character to appear to be stood in the distance in an alleyway, they'll need to have their camera be able to see their whole body in the shot.

Use immersive view to have video backgrounds

As things currently are, you can only add still images as immersive view backgrounds in Zoom. If you would like your stream to feature a video backdrop, one workaround would be to use Zoom with broadcasting software.

When you add the still image in Zoom, just add a solid green colour, and in your broadcasting software use the chroma key/greenscreen effect to remove that colour from the view of the Zoom meeting.

For your audience, they will now only see the cast and the video background that you would like them to see. One drawback however is that the cast will not see the video background and will only see the green colour. This may prove unpleasant on their eyes after a while, so please take this into consideration.

Apps

There are many apps that can be added to Zoom, and these can enhance the look and functionality of your shows.

As a note, you may need to have each user of Zoom install the app on their computer to be able to use or get the benefit of them.

As examples of the kinds of things you can add app wise, you can add onscreen gifs and emojis, drawing tools, timers and even some interactive games. There will be lots of new apps added over time, and these will be things you can explore to see if anything suits the needs of your virtual theatre shows.

II: DESIGNING YOUR SHOW IN GOOGLE MEET

On a computer, you access Google Meet directly from your browser, and for smart device users, you can download an app. For this guide, we'll be looking at the computer-based programme.

Google Meet doesn't currently allow you to directly stream to social media platforms from Google Meet itself. If you wish to use Google Meet as your video meeting software, you will have to screen capture the browser window or desktop view in a separate broadcasting software.

Getting started

Once on the Google Meet website click the 'new meeting' button to get started followed by 'start an instant meeting'. You may be asked to allow access to your webcam and mic, and if so, do this.

As with other video meeting software in this book, I would recommend you either have a friend join the call or join the meeting a second time yourself from another device. This will allow you to see various layout options.

Layout

Assuming you have at least two webcam views in your meeting, click on the three-dot menu from the tools along the bottom of the screen. Choose to change layout and you'll see you have the option for auto, tiles, spotlight and sidebar. The tiled layout may crop some of the participants' webcams as more people are added, so keep this in mind when designing your show around several people being onscreen at once.

Virtual backgrounds

Choose 'apply visual effects' from the three-dot menu and you'll be given the option to blur your background, or replace your background either with one of the stock virtual backgrounds or your own. At the time of writing, Google offer some stock video backgrounds, and whilst you can odd your own image file, you cannot add your own video file as a virtual background.

Whiteboard

You can create a whiteboard which will allow you to draw on the screen, or add in pictures, sticky notes and use a laser pointer to point out things on your whiteboard.

As a note for the whiteboard, keep in mind that the whiteboard will launch as a separate window from your browser. This means that in whichever broadcasting software you are using to stream the view of the video meeting, you either must add the whiteboard as an additional video source, or screen capture the desktop view to show it onscreen. If you just add the browser window as a source to show the Google Meet meeting, it will not automatically capture the whiteboard.

Hide your meeting invite code

If you are the host of the video call and are the person streaming it from your computer, one thing to be aware of is that the meeting's invite code may display on your screen. For me, it was constantly visible in the bottom left corner of the screen next to the current time. As you'll have to screen capture your browser window or desktop view to broadcast the meeting, this would be visible. If people see this whilst you are streaming, you may find you have unwanted strangers attempt to join the meeting.

The solution to any potential gate crashers is to either crop out the view of the invite code or cover it up. As you'll need to use broadcasting software to stream the meeting, check the instructions for designing your show in your chosen broadcasting software to learn how to do this.

Software such as OBS, SLOBS, Twitch Studio and XSplit all easily allow you to crop any elements you add to a show design, and likewise they allow you to add image or video overlays and logos which will obscure the view.

III: DESIGINING YOUR SHOW IN MESSENGER ROOMS FROM FACEBOOK/META

Layout options

Messenger Rooms is limited in what it offers for layout options. You can switch between speaker and grid views, but that's it. I also found that the person running the stream would have their webcam restricted to a smaller size in the bottom corner of the screen. As such I would suggest using Messenger Rooms isn't ideal for creating any virtual theatre shows if the person running the stream is also performing.

Filters

I found that Messenger Rooms would only allow the use of filters and virtual backgrounds for those using smart devices and not on computers at the time of writing. This again limits what the person streaming from their computer can do to be an active part of any show.

To use filters on the smart device Messenger app, tap the screen and you'll see icons for various filters and effects at the top of the screen.

You will see a selection of Snap Chat style face filters which will add virtual hats, hair and other costume and props to the webcam. As a cool feature, you can choose to add these to either just yourself by selecting 'For me' or to all participants by selecting 'For everyone'.

Virtual backgrounds and 360 backgrounds

The virtual backgrounds on Messenger Rooms were some of the more impressive ones available from any of the software tested. In addition to being able to blur your own background and add your own images, videos or animated GIFs, you could also choose from a range of 360 backdrops which move if you move the position of your device.

A 360 virtual background can be used effectively to give a sense that a performer's character is in an actual location. This can be achieved by the performer (or separate camera operator) moving the camera around and the view of the background will adjust to reflect this movement. This effect was only available on smart devices and wouldn't be able to be achieved on a computer with a stationary webcam.

Timer, Polls and Video Clips

If you click the + symbol at the top right of the screen you will bring up several activities that can be added to your video meeting. These include a timer, interactive poll that others in the video call can vote on, and the watch together feature, which allows you to watch video clips in the meeting.

The ability to watch clips with the watch together feature may not be the most useful, as using any video clips you don't own could get your show into copyright issues, unless it could count as fair usage. You can read more about this in the copyright section.

A way to use this feature to good effect would be that you get video clips such as intro sequences, or pre-recorded segments of your show, and upload them to Facebook. You would then be able to search for the clips or add them to your saved for later list to be able to quickly show them.

As you cannot stream to social media platforms directly from the Messenger Rooms software you will need to use a broadcasting software to capture your Messenger video call. As such, the watch together feature wouldn't be the best method to display intro sequences in your show, as most broadcasting software can handle it better.

It would still be useful if you needed to play a clip for the other performers to see, as showing clips this way displays them better than if you were to use the screenshare option.

Screensharing

You can quickly choose to screenshare a display monitor or open window on your computer by clicking the screenshare option from the menu at the bottom centre of your screen. Doing this will show your monitor in full screen mode to other callers, but will relegate the screenshare image to the bottom corner of the screen for the person who shared it. This will also replace the view of the webcam of the person who shared it, so this is problematic if they need to be seen in the show at the same time.

IV: DESIGNING YOUR SHOW IN SKYPE (ON COMPUTER)

Once you are signed into Skype, you'll want to start a meeting so you can see the programme as it'll look with other people in the video call. You can either set a meeting up with a friend to help you out (even if they just leave their webcam on – you don't need them to do anything) or just use a smart phone to connect as a second account.

From the left panel choose 'Meet Now' and then host a meeting. This will create a video meeting. Copy the link and send it to your friend/yourself to get two or more people in the meeting room.

Theme and Appearance Customisation

You'll now want to access the appearance settings, which can be accessed from the three-lines menu at the top left corner of the screen. This will open the lefthand side panel where you can click the three-dot menu at the top and choose settings.

Opening the side panel during a show will reveal your contact list on screen, so I would suggest setting things up before your show. A shortcut to access the settings menu is to press the control and comma keys on your keyboard.

When the settings pop up enter the appearance tab. Here you will be able change the colour of text boxes, and switch between light and dark modes. At the time of writing these were the only things I could change in the appearance tab on my computer.

Layout and Together Mode

You can swap between speaker view and grid view to change the layout from just the current person speaking to a split view of everyone.

In grid view, you can click on the three-dot menu next to a participant's name and toggle between Fit and Crop video and See Full Video. This will zoom in on the videos to fill the whole screen and not leave black bars around each webcam feed.

Together mode is like Immersive view on Zoom and will place meeting participants into a virtual set. Once selected you can choose to change scene and are given several options of scenes to choose from. I didn't find that there was a way to currently change the scene to an image of your choosing which is a shame, but it wouldn't surprise me if this was added at a later date.

Note that together mode will remove the background from behind each participant, so they look more naturally part of the scene they have been added to. This will mean that any virtual backgrounds you have selected will not be displayed.

As a last note I found that whilst in together mode the window showing the meeting was slightly reduced in size and would display a bar along the top of the meeting to show the participants. Even entering full screen mode didn't remove this, so if you wanted to use together mode in your show, you may have to accept this displays or crop this out when importing your Skype call into your broadcasting software.

Virtual Backgrounds

Virtual backgrounds are added by each individual user and can be changed by going to the three-dot menu next to your name and selecting change background. Skype offers a range of images, or you can upload your own. As things are at the time of writing, you can only add images and not video backgrounds.

V: DESIGNING YOUR SHOW IN MICROSOFT TEAMS

Before you begin

At the time of writing, Microsoft Teams doesn't offer any way to broadcast the video meeting to social media platforms from within Teams itself. You will still be able to use Teams as the video meeting place for your cast, but will have to use a separate broadcasting software such as OBS, SLOBS or Twitch Studio to send the video feed to YouTube etc.

Getting started

Once you've signed in, click 'Meet' to set up your video meeting, and then select meet now. You can schedule meetings, and this may be a useful way to send out invite links in advance, but just for now, so we can familiarise ourselves with the tools click meet now.

Layout of participants

The options of how to arrange the participants in a Microsoft Teams meeting are limited. At the time of writing, this is what I found you could achieve/could not achieve.

The webcam of the host will be small on screen

Regardless of whether you use the computer app, or mobile app, I found that from the perspective of each user that your webcam view would be relegated to being small and in the corner of the screen. This is problematic if you are the host of the Teams meeting and intend to appear onscreen in the virtual theatre show.

A workaround to this issue would be that the host join the meeting twice. Once, on their computer that will handle the stream, and from a separate device, such as a smartphone or tablet. Doing this would allow you to be seen in a larger window as a separate participant.

If you do this, I'd suggest you switch your computer camera off and minimize the window by selecting the three-dot menu next to your name and choosing 'Hide for me'.

Spotlighting Participants

To spotlight one or more participants, click the three-dot menu next to their name and select add spotlight. You can also choose to 'pin for me' which will effectively spotlight a person, but they will not appear spotlighted for the other performers in the meeting.

Together mode

Together mode allows the participants in the meeting to be placed into a virtual scene. This is a feature also available in Skype and is like immersive mode from Zoom.

You can choose to change the scene and there are several scenes preloaded for you to pick from.

There is also an option to create your own scene, but in my time with the software, I found this asked me to sign in to the Microsoft website, but wouldn't let me with a personal account. If you want to access this feature, it would seem you need a work or school account. This will limit many people from being able to access this feature.

Virtual backgrounds

Click the more button at the top of the meeting and select apply background effects. A panel will appear on the right of the screen and let you choose to either blur your background or add a virtual one. You can even add your own image.

Note that Microsoft Teams allows you to add image files but doesn't currently allow you to add video backgrounds.

Screenshare

Click the share button from the options at the top of the screen and you will be able to select from any monitor displays or application windows you have open on your computer.

In my tests of the software, I found that the screen you wish to share will only be shared to the screens of the other participants and will not display in the preview window of the meeting on your own computer.

This means that the person streaming the show cannot effectively display what they wish to screenshare on a broadcast. A solution to this would be that a different person screenshare anything that may need to be screenshared during your show, but obviously created the issue of sharing the responsibilities of doing the tech work on the show.

VI: DESIGNING YOUR SHOW ON IN OBS AND SLOBS

Before we begin

If you have jumped right to this section, we're now going to discuss how to design your show in OBS and SLOBS. If you haven't done so, I would suggest you familiarise yourself with Zoom or another video meeting software first, as you'll need to use one of these with the broadcasting software.

For this part of the guide, I will give instructions based around the experience of using OBS, although the experience of using Stream Labs OBS is very very similar (at time of writing).

Getting started

Once you have your broadcasting software open, in this instance OBS, you will see an empty black rectangle which represents the blank canvas where your stream will be created. As you add elements to the canvas, if they are visible in this area, they will be visible to your viewers.

You will also notice the tool bar at the top of the screen, and sections for the Audio Mixer, Scenes, Sources and Controls. Take a note of these as these controls will be what you use to design and run your show.

Create some scenes

Under the scenes tab, you'll see controls to add or remove a scene. Click add, and I would suggest you add the following scenes:

- Pre-Show
- Live Show
- Interval/Be Right Back
- End of Show
- Technical Difficulties

Once these are added and named, you will need to go through each one and add the elements you want the audience to be able to see and hear during the show.

The Pre-Show

Now you have a blank Pre-Show scene I would suggest you add the following basic elements.

A company logo/Show logo

To do this, I'll assume you have a company logo and have it saved somewhere on your hard drive. As a tip, I would suggest you save the image in the PNG format and have the logo on a transparent background. This can be made in your art software and will look more professional than if your logo has a box around it for the sake of it.

To add the logo, go to the sources tab and click the add/plus symbol. Choose to add an image, and when prompted, name the source as 'Logo'. Choose the file from your hard drive, and when it loads you can resize and reposition the logo to wherever you want on the screen.

As a further tip it may be worth ticking the box to 'unload image when not showing' from the pop-up menu for the file. This will help keep the speed of the software faster as the computer won't have the strain of every on-screen element being loaded into the computer's memory, even when it's not displaying.

If the object you add comes up much bigger than the preview window, here's an easy way to shrink it down. Right click onto the object you've just added (graphic/video etc) and from the menu that comes up hover over the word 'Transform'. When the next set of options pops up click on 'fit to screen' and the object will be resized to size of the canvas area. If you're adding a video or background this may now be the perfect size, but if it's still too big, just go to the corner of the object you've added and drag it down to size and reposition it where you need it.

A still, or video background

Now the logo is added, just repeat the process of clicking the add symbol and this time choose a 'Media Source' if you wish to add a video background.

Choose the file form your hard drive. When loading any media files make sure you check the box for the 'loop' option if you are adding the file as a video background. If not, the file will play once and then not be visible.

Once it's loaded resize it to what works for you. If the video appears in front of the logo, simply go to the sources tab, and drag whichever elements need to be displayed on top to the top of the list.

You will also note that there are icons that look like an eye and a lock next to each item on the list. Clicking the eye will change each element from being visible to invisible, and this will be a control that is useful to know if you are running the tech during the live stream. If you click the lock symbol, it will lock the size and position of the element and prevent you from accidentally moving an item by mistake.

On screen text

Under source, click add and then choose Text (GDI+) and it will bring up a menu where you can type or paste in text. You'll also be able to change the font, and colour of the text.

Text that is useful to write may include information about the show, such as the start time and where people can watch it. Other information that may be worth adding could be the company website or names of the cast/crew involved.

Once this is typed, you can move around the text box and resize it just like any other element.

Music

Once again click add and pick 'media source' and this time choose the music file you wish to play as background music for this pre-show screen. As with the video background, make sure you click to loop the music if you want the same music to continuously play during the pre-show.

A microphone input

This one is optional, as you may not feel it is useful to include the ability to add voice over to a pre-show screen. The reason I would recommend it, is because if your show is running late, or if there is another issue and you need to communicate with your audience, having access to talk directly to them is very handy.

Your first scene is ready!

These are all the basic elements you need for the pre-show screen. Now you know how to add these elements and create this scene, creating further scenes is very much the same. As such, I'll take a less step by step approach and instead highlight what the elements you need are, why you need them and only guide you through the process of adding things if we've not already covered it.

Live Show

This will be your main scene where the audience will watch the performance.

Adding in the view of your video meeting

The most important part of this scene is the view of your video meeting. I suggest you add this to the scene first and then add everything else around it. I'll use Zoom as the example for adding a video meeting in, but the process remains the same if you are using Skype, Microsoft Teams etc

In order to add Zoom or whatever video meeting software to the stream, you must open that software. So open Zoom and start a meeting so you can see a preview of the Zoom call.

Back in OBS, add a new source, and choose 'Window Capture'. Name it Zoom and when the properties menu comes up it will show a preview. Underneath the preview there is a drop-down menu called Window – from here select Zoom.exe and you should see your Zoom call come up in the preview box.

Before you click OK, you'll see that you can either check a box to capture your mouse cursor or not. Depending on your show, you may want to use the mouse cursor as part of the show as a pointer, or if you don't have a use for it, make sure it's unchecked. Once you've decided, click OK and your Zoom window will now be in your stream.

Let's talk about the size of your Zoom window

Here's a decision you'll have to make at some point. What size do you want your Zoom window to take up on the screen? Once you've added the Zoom meeting, you could choose to fit it to the size of the canvas and be done with.

If you want your performers seen, and don't want to add any logos or other effects, you are nearly done. If you want to add logos, add a frame to your show, or add an onscreen chat box, we have several more things to cover.

But even if you just want the Zoom window to take up full screen, there is one more major point to consider.

The size and view of Zoom will change in your stream if you alter the size of the Zoom programme whilst using it.

Let's say you've added the view of Zoom to your project in OBS already. Now go over to Zoom and try either clicking maximize or restore down (same button as maximize) in the top right area of the Zoom window. You'll notice that the size of the Zoom meeting in OBS will adjust. This may be a little or it may be a lot.

As a further experiment, try dragging the corner of the Zoom window to stretch it so it's long but not tall. The results will be that in OBS the Zoom call is displayed as a small box and there are black bars either side of the view of the zoom meeting.

The point is that even once you've added your video call into the design of your stream, the size you have the programme open as outside of OBS will affect how it is displayed in OBS.

The easy solution to this is to just have the Zoom call maximised right?

Not quite. That will work to some degree, but let's throw another spanner into the works.

Back in the Zoom programme, hover the mouse over the screen to see the controls along the bottom. Click on either participants or chat, and the screen will adjust to show you a panel to the right of your meeting view. In this window it will show a list of any participants and display the chat between yourself and any participants on the call.

Now check OBS, and you'll see that the side panel of the chat and participants is also shown on screen on your stream. This can feel like a disaster as it not only takes up a healthy chunk of real estate of your screen but will also reveal any private chat between cast and crew and effectively give your audience a view backstage of your show!

Fear not.

I'm going to make the assumption that everyone in the call may need access to the call's chat in case of issues, or more specifically, that the person who is streaming the show from their computer may also be the host or co-host of the meeting and need to access the chat or participant's window.

If this is the case, you will have the issue of the chat window displaying on your screen, and we need to fix that.

An easy solution is that everyone in the show use Facebook Messenger, or some other group chat to communicate, but this won't allow access to the participants panel.

The better solution in my books, would be to either resize/crop the window showing the Zoom meeting in OBS, or to use overlay elements to hide the chat from the audience's view. I'll cover how to add overlays shortly.

If you resize the Zoom meeting in OBS, you can just drag the corner of the Zoom window until the side panel isn't visible anymore.

Cropping elements in OBS

If you wish to crop the window, this is how it's done.

Right click either the onscreen element you wish to crop, or the name of it from the list under sources. Then choose filters, and when the pop-up menu appears choose the + symbol to add a filter and choose crop/pad. Now simply adjust the numbers for the left, top, right and bottom of the element to cut what is visible.

Making sure audio is set up correctly

Now we have the Zoom meeting (or other video meeting) visible in OBS, you need to make sure the audience can hear everyone as well as see everyone.

If you look to the audio mixer tab on OBS, you should see that desktop audio is present as one of the sources.

If it isn't, go to the sources tab and click the + symbol and choose Audio Output Capture. From here select the name of your computer's speaker.

There will be a slider to adjust the volume that the audio will come through to the audience. In chapter 21 we'll talk about sound checks for volume, but first we need to make sure we are getting audio come through at all.

The easiest way to check this is to play music or hop over to YouTube and play a video – anything that makes sound that you can hear through your computer's speakers. As this music/other sound is playing take a look at the Audio Mixer on OBS and you should see the volume metre jumping about to show that it is picking up any sounds that are played through your computer.

Making sure you can be heard on your stream

Here comes the tricky part where newcomers may run into an issue.

Once you have added your video meeting to the canvas in OBS/SLOBS, look at the audio mixer and you may notice that as other people talk, you will see the volume metre jump about under desktop audio. If you speak however, you will notice that the volume metre doesn't move for desktop audio.

The reason for this is because Zoom will take the audio of you speaking and play it to the other participants in the meeting but will not play the sound of you speaking through your own computer. If it did you would constantly hear an echo of yourself. The Desktop audio will feature the voices of literally everyone else on the Zoom call, but not the person running OBS to stream the show.

The solution to this is simple...almost.

Just as we spoke about when adding an audio input source in the pre-show section, if you want your voice to be heard by the audience, you'll have to add your microphone into this scene.

Under source, click the + symbol and choose audio input capture, name your mic and choose your best quality microphone. This will enable the audience to hear the clearest audio from you.

Simple right?

Well, there may be one final issue. If the microphone you've just added is the same microphone you use in Zoom, there is a chance that the software won't allow you to use the same mic for two applications at the same time. Some people have this issue and others don't, but let's say how to resolve it just in case.

Head back into the Zoom application and in the bottom left corner there will be the microphone controls. There will be the picture of the mic, which if clicked will mute your mic. Next to it there will be a little arrow ^ which if you click will bring up the audio input and output settings in Zoom.

In OBS you will have chosen your best microphone so the audience can hear you clearly, and now in Zoom just make sure you choose a different microphone, and this will be used for your fellow performers or crew to hear you. This mic needs to be good enough quality so that the other people in the Zoom meeting can hear you, but if it's lower quality that isn't the end of the world as the audience won't hear it.

As an example, In OBS I set my microphone to my Elgato Wave: 3, and in Zoom I select my microphone as 'Microphone (Realtek High-Definition Audio)' which is my computer's built-in mic.

By having separate mics between your video call and your broadcasting software you avoid them conflicting with each other.

Overlays

Overlays are graphics or videos which you place on top of other elements. These may include logos, or frames/borders, or your social media live chat window. Depending on your show and what you feel fits presentation wise, you may decide to include lots, few or none of these.

For the purpose of this section, we'll assume you want several things, and talk you through what they are and how to implement them.

A frame/border for your Zoom meeting

You want your show to be eye catching, and if it just looks like a Zoom meeting, this won't stand out to potential audience who just happen by it.

A frame or border can give your show an element of presentation, just as stage curtains or lights add to the atmosphere of a theatre.

If you want to add a static border, just add a PNG image of the border with the centre section as a transparent area shaped to match the size of your zoom meeting.

If you want to add a video border, follow the same steps as discussed in the pre-show section to add a video background. Under the source tab, click the + symbol, choose media source and choose your video. Make sure you click for the video to loop, otherwise your border will disappear when the video ends.

Unlike adding PNG image files which can have transparent areas, the process to add a transparent video overlay is slightly more complicated.

Video files such as MP4 or AVI files cannot have transparent areas like a PNG image file. Instead, you'll either need to source or create a video of your frame, and make sure the background of the frame is a solid colour, such as green. Then you can remove the colour in OBS like removing a green screen.

Let's look at how removing green screens work in OBS so we can apply it to any element that we wish to display as a cut out shape.

Removing Green Screens

To remove a green screen, you need to use an effect known as a 'chroma key'. Once you've added the overlay (or other element) that has a green background, right click the overlay and choose filters.

Click + to add a new filter and choose chroma key. A menu will pop up and you'll be able to choose which colour you wish to remove. The basic options are green, blue or magenta, but you'll also see 'Custom' where you can pick any colour you want.

The other tools below the colour selection will allow you to adjust the strength of the effect and will also allow you to change the opacity of the layer, which will allow the border, or logo etc to display slightly see through. This may be useful for logos in particular, for an effect like you get on many TV channels where you see a channel logo faintly in a corner.

Adding an overlay of your chat window

If you've ever seen people stream video games, you may have noticed that they often will feature an area of the screen where you see the Twitch, or YouTube chat just scrolling on the screen. You may wonder why they would want this, and question why you may want this if you are running a virtual theatre performance.

Reasons not to have it include that having your audience chat displayed would be like your in person audience chatting in the front row. It may be distracting for other audience members. Another reason not to have it would be because the chat would be baked into the video of the show. So, if any audience members were rude that would be on the video of your show...forever.

So, what are the reasons to have it? If you have the chat window displayed as part of the video it means that audience members can get a sense of each other's excitement for the show, and this can help encourage more people to watch longer or engage in the chat. When it comes to growing your audience, this can be very useful.

The other reason to display the chat is so you can display a combined chat from multiple social media platforms. Services like Restream or StreamYard allow you combine a chat window of messages that come from various social media platforms like YouTube, Twitch, Facebook etc. If you have an aggregated chat box displayed on the stream, your audience members will be able to see what each other are saying and even reply to each other even if they're not using the same platform.

It could also encourage users on one platform to hop across and watch on another. Say you've just started your stream and there are 25 people watching and chatting on Twitch, and 10 watching and chatting on Facebook, but only 2 watching and chatting on YouTube. The 2 viewers on YouTube may feel that people aren't interested in your show and may decide to give up watching. If they can see the combined chat and notice that there are lots of people chatting back and forth on other social media channels, they might decide to head over and join the busier chat, which may help them feel a bigger part of the community around your show.

Adding a combined chat via Restream

If you're using the Restream service, you'll have to log in to their website and click on 'set up your stream'. On the next page you'll see a tab that says 'Chat'. Click this and from here choose the chat overlay option which will bring up a web link which you should copy.

Now head back over to OBS and under the sources tab, click the + symbol. This time choose 'browser' and click OK. Now paste the URL from the Restream site into the URL textbox and click OK.

You'll see the chat box appear in your stream. You can now position it wherever you feel it would be best placed – I usually have mine to the right side of the screen. If it appears too large/tall/wide simply double-click on the browser under the source tab and you'll be able to set the size.

Stream Labs OBS offer a chat box widget which will allow you to display your chat messages on the stream. This works exactly the same way as Restream where you set it up on the Stream Labs website, and then can copy a URL to past into a Browser source in OBS, SLOBS etc.

Additional scenes

By now, you should have a pre-show scene and live show scene set up, but there are a couple of other important scenes you could consider setting up. These are:

Interval/Be Right Back

End of Show

Technical Difficulties

Setting these up will follow all the same steps as setting up the pre-show and live show, so let's just talk about the purpose of each scene.

Interval/Be Right Back

It's useful to have an Interval scene as a way to let the audience know that the cast are taking a short break but will be right back in a few minutes.

End of Show Scene

This scene would let the audience know that the current performance has finished, and you could thank the audience for their support. You could also take the opportunity to display your web links, or a video/picture advert to let the audience know what other projects you have coming up.

Technical Difficulties Scene

Tech issues happen all the time with streaming shows. A performer may lose internet connection, or someone's mic may fail. If you run into a tech issue which means the action of the show has to take a pause, it could be useful to create a Technical Difficulties screen. You can use this to inform the audience that there is an issue, but that you are working hard to resolve it quickly.

In theory these could all be the same scene as the pre-show, and you could just switch on/off text or graphics to change the message from 'Starting soon' to 'Interval: Be back soon' or 'Technical difficulties' etc.

This is a useful opportunity to talk about switching elements of your stream on/off.

Turning stream elements on/off

There are times in your shows that you may wish to display an element for a short time, but not want it permanently displayed onscreen. This could be an advert for something, a timer, or a graphic of a set/prop to create atmosphere for a location in a play.

To switch an element on/off in your stream just look at the sources tab in OBS and you'll see the eye icon next to the lock icon. Simply click on the eye to toggle things between being visible and invisible.

If you have a Stream Deck you can assign any of your stream sources to buttons for easy access to switch them on/off. Using a device such as a Stream Deck will mean you can avoid the hassle of having to always having to scroll through what may be small text to find each element you wish to turn off.

Lastly, you could choose to assign hotkeys to each source. By doing this you can toggle elements on/off with the press of a button on your keyboard.

Assigning hotkeys in OBS/SLOBS

To assign hotkeys in OBS/SLOBS click on settings and then choose hotkeys from the pop-up window. Now scroll through the list of all the sources in your scene and find the source you wish to add hotkeys to. Now simply highlight the textbox and press the key on your keyboard that you wish to toggle that source with.

Plugins

There are countless plugins that you can get to achieve almost anything you could want within a stream created in OBS. In Stream Labs you'll need to look for addons and widgets from the Stream Labs team and therefore are fewer options.

I won't be able to walk you through how to implement everything as there are literally thousands of plugins made by the streaming community, but here are a few examples of ideas you could explore to implement.

Highlight Comments

It's possible to highlight a specific comment that a viewer has written in the chat. This would be handy during an improv show where you may ask for audience suggestions, or during Q&A sessions.

Scoreboard

If you're producing a gameshow or competitive stand up, dance or singing show, you may benefit from having an onscreen scoreboard to help performers and viewers keep track.

Tip jar

An onscreen element which will highlight any donations/tips your viewers have given to you throughout the stream.

Spin wheel

If your company is running any kind of competition or needs to select something at random, you could find some use from a spin wheel. This will allow you to randomly select a name, or other item from a list you input.

Using your webcam in OBS/SLOBS without using Zoom

Let's say your project is a one person show, a podcast, or that you're filming multiple people on stage and streaming that via OBS. In any of these scenarios you wouldn't need a to use a video conferencing software such as Zoom or Skype and could just use your webcam directly with the broadcasting software.

To do this, click the + symbol under sources and select video capture device. When the pop-up window appears just choose the name of your attached webcam and you will see the video feed come through into OBS.

VII: DESIGNING YOUR SHOW ON STREAMYARD

Once you've signed up and created your account on StreamYard, click on the broadcasts section of the site and it'll ask you to create a broadcast.

Choose broadcast destinations (If you haven't connected StreamYard to social media platforms, you can do this from the destinations tab) and choose to enter the studio.

When entering the studio, I would suggest you switch on your webcam, and that if possible, you either invite a friend to join you, or simply send the invite link to your phone/tablet and enter the room a second time on that device. The reason for this, is so that you can see what the screen will look like with a minimum of two people on the screen.

Having just one person in the studio will make it so you can only see what their webcam looks like at full screen, and not see the various layouts and background options.

You can get a limited preview of what the backgrounds will look like with just one person in the show, and to do this click on settings, and under layouts, check the box for 'Crop solo layout to show background images'.

Once you have two webcams visible, you'll be able to explore how the different views look and how controlling them work. For now, let's continue designing your show in StreamYard.

Viewer Comments

A great function of StreamYard is that it makes it easy to display viewer comments on the stream. This is useful for audience interactive shows and it is easy to toggle the display of messages on/off.

To do this, click on the comments tab from the menu panel on the right. You will see the chat messages displayed, and to highlight one on the show, just click on the message and it will pop up on the bottom of the screen. It will display the comment and the profile pic of the person who commented in a slick professional style, but you won't have the ability to change the position or layout of the comment.

If during a show, you see some comments that you want to come back to later, you can easily hover over a comment and click to 'star' a comment, and then you'll be able to find any starred comments from the top of the comments box from the starred tab.

Banners

From the menu panel on the right of the screen, choose banners, and you'll be able to create banners for display at the bottom of the screen. These can say anything you'd like, but are useful to display messages to remind viewers to subscribe or when your next show is on.

Once created just click on the banner you want to display to toggle it on or off.

Brand

The Brand tab from the side panel will give you the most options to customise the design of your show in StreamYard. Once selected you'll be able to change various elements of the look of your show.

As a nice feature, at the top of the menu it will display the name of the brand that you are editing, and if you click the name, you'll be given the option to create new brands or choose ones you've already created. This is a good feature if you have multiple shows that you want to select between.

Brand colour

This option allows you to pick a colour that will change the background colour to any onscreen names or banners.

Theme

The theme will change the display style and animation of the pop-up banners.

Logo

The logo option will allow you to add a custom logo for display in the corner of your stream. If you use a PNG of GIF file, you can add an image with a transparent background. This will mean the logo doesn't have to be square or rectangular and can be a cut out shape.

Overlay

This will allow you to add a border or frame as a layer over your background and webcam views. This is useful to give your show more brand recognition, or to add overlays that reflect the atmosphere or location of your scenes.

Overlays are only available for paid subscribers of StreamYard, and whilst you can create multiple overlays, you can only use one at a time. This means that you'll have to lock any elements you want in your overlay onto a single image.

Overlays will also need to be saved as PNG or GIF files and have transparent areas so that your webcams can be seen. As the overlay sits on top of your webcam and background layers, it will mask anything underneath it unless you leave transparent spaces.

You can either source free overlays online, create a custom one yourself or have someone make one for you.

A note on overlays is that you cannot use video elements as overlays (at the time of writing) like you can achieve in other software we have covered in this book.

Video clips

Whilst you may not be able to use video overlays to frame your stream, you can use pre-recorded video clips on StreamYard. You can upload videos and play them by clicking on them once uploaded. These can be useful for intro videos, or end credits, countdown timers, or if you had any scenes that you wanted to include that needed to be shot in advance.

Background music

StreamYard offer a selection of music you can play that won't interfere with copyright issues on social media platforms. For more information on copyright and your show, check the copyright section later in the book in chapter 17.

Screensharing

An alternative to uploading clips from the branding menu is to use the Share option. This will allow you to share your screen, slides, an additional camera, or a video file.

I wouldn't recommend you upload video clips in this way, as they loaded very slow in my testing. As such I would suggest you upload any clips under the brand tab, and not via the share option.

Sharing an additional camera view would be useful for two people in the same room, or if you want to show an overhead camera or wider shot.

Screensharing your desktop can be an easier way to show video clips, images, a video game or a computer tutorial. You can do screenshare with just one screen, but it's better if you have a second monitor to screenshare from.

If you have just one screen, you'll have to have what you are sharing on top of the view of StreamYard, which means you won't be able to see and interact with your own stream anymore.

Using StreamYard with other broadcasting software

StreamYard has several nice features to offer, but it is limited when compared to something like OBS, which we have covered in detail already. It is possible to use StreamYard as an alternative to Zoom, and get some of these benefits.

If you want to benefit from cropped view split screen, customisable backgrounds and such like, or just like the StreamYard interface, here's how you can get the best of both worlds. As a warning, to do this, this method is a workaround and does create some challenges.

For best results you'll need to have at least two monitors connected to your computer, and the idea is that you'll stream through your broadcasting software and use the StreamYard Studio simply as a meeting place for your team in a similar way to how you would use Zoom. You wouldn't be streaming live directly from StreamYard.

As a note, whilst you may gain some features when using StreamYard in this way, you would also lose some. These include the ability to get the onscreen comments pop up, as you would need to stream through StreamYard for this to function. You may also have to share some tech responsibilities with another member of your team or rely on hotkeys for some functions, but we'll explore this later.

Here's how it's done:

In StreamYard

Log in to StreamYard. Once your team have assembled do not press to go live. You won't be doing that from here.

In your broadcasting software

Now open your broadcasting software. For this example, we'll be using OBS, but the same principle will work for any of them.

Under the sources tab click the +/add symbol and choose display capture. Now choose the display where you have StreamYard displayed. As a note, you'll need to have StreamYard on a monitor that you don't use for other tasks, because if you have other windows open on the same screen as you are capturing the display of, they would be visible on your stream on top of what you are trying to capture.

Designing your stream in your broadcasting software on top of StreamYard

Now you should have StreamYard Studio visible in your broadcasting software. StreamYard will now function in place of importing your Zoom meeting into OBS. This view of StreamYard is now the base canvas for which you can add other layers on top.

Please refer to the 'Designing your show in OBS' section for how to add layers over your Zoom meeting/other video meeting.

You could now add video borders/frames on top of your StreamYard meeting, or anything else you can add as a layer in OBS which is not possible in StreamYard alone.

A note about running StreamYard as a video source through other broadcasting software

You are likely to find some challenges when using StreamYard in this way. If you have StreamYard in full screen mode, you can no longer access all the controls that are normally visible in StreamYard Studio. This includes the brand and banners tab and the layout controls.

The easiest solution to this is to share the tech work with another person. When you log into StreamYard, and before you go into the Studio, you can go to the members tab. Here you can invite and assign other people to be team members in admin or co-host roles. People with these roles will have the ability to change the layout and display banners.

If you do not have someone who can take on some of these responsibilities, there is one other solution I'd recommend. StreamYard has the function where you can set hotkeys. If you have full screen mode displayed and need to change the layout or do a range of other functions, you can set a key on your keyboard to fulfil the same role. It's not as intuitive, but if you have a Stream Deck or similar device, you could set this up to make it easier.

VIII: DESIGNING YOUR SHOW IN RESTREAM STUDIO

Many people will just use Restream's multi-streaming service. When used in conjunction with other broadcasting software it allows you to multi-stream your videos to several social media platforms at once. Restream also offer Restream Studio, which allows you to create and stream broadcasts directly from your browser.

Once logged in, click to enter Restream Studio. In the centre of the screen, you will see a preview of your stream. To the left you will see a list of participants and their camera preview and to the right are the tools to edit the design of the show.

I would suggest that before you start editing the design of your show, that you invite a guest into the meeting so you can test the controls and see the look of your show with multiple participants involved. This doesn't have to be an actual person, as you can just use a smart device as the second camera to test things.

In the right panel you will see tabs for chat, captions and graphics. We'll begin with graphics.

Theme

Theme will allow you to change the presentation of the names and captions that appear on screen. You can also choose a colour for these graphics.

Logo

You can add PNG or GIF images as logos, and these will appear with transparent backgrounds in the top right corner of the screen.

Overlay

The overlay feature will allow you to upload image overlays to add a frame or border to your show. You may upload multiple designs, but you can only use one at a time and cannot stack them. Once loaded, you also cannot move, resize or adjust the images.

You will also need to have an overlay image with a transparent centre to allow a space to show your meeting participants.

Creating additional scenes via the Brand folder

In the top right corner of the screen, you will see the brand folder. If you click on it, you will have the option to create new brands. These are useful if you have multiple shows or brands and want to create separate virtual sets for each.

They can also be used to effectively create multiple scenes as you can do in other broadcasting software.

Using overlays as additional scenes

As an alternative to using the brand folder to create new scenes, you could use full screen overlays to fulfil the purpose of a 'be right back' screen or technical difficulties screen.

Video Clips

Click the + symbol to add a video clip which can be played by selecting it once uploaded. These can be useful for show intros, or promo videos. When you click to play the video clip, your mics will be muted.

Backgrounds

Restream allow you to upload video backgrounds which will play on loop.

Captions

Captions is the tab next to graphics and allows you to bring up prewritten messages that you may wish to call upon during a show. Things like please subscribe would be useful to create.

Chat

The final tab in the right-hand panel is the chat tab. Restream have a really good aggregated chat function, and with the chat tab open you'll be able to read and reply to any messages that come through on social media platforms that you are connected to.

If you want to highlight a comment, it is as simple as clicking on the message and it will display at the bottom of the stream.

You also have the option to add the chat as an overlay on the right-hand side of your stream. To toggle this on/off just click on 'chat overlay'. As a unique feature of Restream Studio, the chat overlay won't just overlay the guests in the meeting and will shift them to display smaller on the left side of the screen. This is a neat feature, but does limit the amount of screen that can be used for the performers in your virtual theatre show if you want to have the chat featured on screen at the same time.

Screensharing

In the tools that are just under the stream preview window there is the option to screenshare. If clicked you will be given the choice of choosing to share any monitors you have connected, or any application window you have open. This could be a website, a video game, or another application.

If added to the screen, this will appear in a large window on your stream, whilst any visible participants will appear in small windows to the right.

Background music

Lastly for the design in Restream Studio, you can click the + symbol from the bottom menu of tools and add various sources to your stream. If you select 'Background music' you will be given a selection of background music to choose from that will play at low volume as not to overpower the volume of your mics.

IX: DESIGNING YOUR SHOW IN TWITCH STUDIO

NOTE: As a note before we go further, Twitch Studio is designed to stream directly to Twitch and doesn't offer options to stream to other platforms.

Before we get started

Whilst we'll be using Twitch Studio to broadcast our virtual show, we'll still need to use a video conferencing software at the same time to get our actors on the virtual stage. So, before you begin setting up the stream, you'll need to start a meeting in your video conferencing software. For this tutorial I will be using Zoom, but the same principals will apply whichever software you use for your video call.

Getting started

Once you've downloaded and installed the Twitch Studio software, launch it and you'll have to log in with your Twitch account.

Once in the studio, you'll be presented with the standard layout of the software. In the centre will be the blank canvas where we will create the show. To the left of the canvas is the list of scenes you create, and where you will edit them, and to the right are panels for the stream's activity feed and chat.

Create some scenes

Click the +/add Scene button, and a menu will be shown where you can choose to create scenes from a template or a blank scene. I would recommend creating the following:

- Pre-show
- Live Show
- Be Right Back/Interval
- Technical difficulties

When created, all scenes are named Blank Scene. You can double click on them to rename them.

Editing a scene

Let's look how to create your live show scene first. Before you get started, make sure you have your video call meeting software open. For this example, I'll be using Zoom.

Once the scenes are created, you can hover over their name and select to edit them.

Note that there are controls at the top of the preview window for cropping and cutting etc. We'll come to these later.

Adding layers

For now, go to the left panel and click add layer. From the options that come up choose screen share and click add.

In the right-hand panel, you'll see where it says screen share source. Underneath this, click change and choose your video meeting software from the list of open applications. As I am using Zoom, I chose Zoom.exe. Once selected, you'll have the option to toggle if you want the cursor captured or not. For Extreme Improv shows, I don't mind having the pointer visible as I find it useful, so I have this checked. Now click done to add it to your show.

Customising your design

Now you can see your Zoom meeting in the preview, you have the option to customise it in several ways.

Resize elements

You can resize the meeting by dragging the corner. You can also use the tools in the panel on the right side of the canvas to change the size and position if you don't want to drag it with a mouse.

You can lock the size and position of an object by clicking the lock icon in the size and position tab.

If you are using Zoom, remember to open the chat and participants panel in the Zoom application so it doesn't surprise you and resize your window later.

Cropping elements

Using Zoom's chat box as an example of something I would want to crop in my stream, select the crop tool from above the stream preview window. You can now drag the corners to whatever size you need and click confirm to crop. If you make an error, just select the tool again and press reset.

Add a border

You can select to add a border to any element you've added. This can be edited to have different colours, thickness and how rounded it is. As an alternative to using overlays for borders this is quite handy, but not as customisable as one crafted as an overlay.

Adding overlays

Now you have your video meeting in the show design, let's add overlays to add custom image and video elements to the design.

Logo/image layers

Click add layer and choose image. Once done, on the right of the screen you can choose to browse for an image file. I would suggest using a PNG or GIF that has a transparent background for this.

Once selected drag the image to where you want it and resize it if need be.

If you are adding a company or show logo, you may want to reduce the opacity of the image, so it is slightly see through. This tool can be found in the edit panel on the right.

Linked Layers

If you have an element that you would like to appear in every scene, you can create linked layers in Twitch Studio. In the right-hand panel under the tab for linked layers, click the small icon (it's a chain link) to link the layers.

Now, when you edit a different scene, click add layer and choose the same layer type as the linked layer – in this example it's an image. When you click the word image, you will notice that the option for 'Existing Linked Layer' will be there. Click on it, and the layer you set up in the previous scene will appear in this one as well.

Just as a warning, if you adjust the design of the layer in the second scene, it will also adjust it in the original scene as well.

Adding video elements

Click to add a layer and choose media. Now on the right panel click browse to find the video file you wish to import.

Once it's loaded, you can edit the size, and other design aspects such as border, cropping etc.

Greenscreen effect

If you want to have a video border, you will need to edit the video in a video editing programme (or have one made for you) and make sure that any space around or inside the border displays a solid colour such as green. This colour can then be removed in Twitch Studio by using the greenscreen effect, leaving you with a nice video border which is transparent to show your video meeting in the centre.

Adding onscreen text

Click add layer and choose text. On the right panel you'll be able to type in whatever text you want to display, and adjust the font, colour, and sizing.

Adding a countdown timer

You can easily add a countdown timer to your scene. This would be useful for a pre-show scene to indicate how long until a stream starts. You can adjust the design, and length of the timer in the right-hand panel. The timer can also be started, paused, and reset from this menu as well.

Adding a chat box

Add a layer and choose chat box. When added, you can position the chat box to where you would like it. I usually position it to the right side of the screen and sized so it's the height of the screen, but only about a fifth or sixth of the width.

You can add test messages from the panel on the right and this will help you decide if you need to resize the text, want a border, or to display solid or with lowered opacity.

Additional scenes

Everything we have discussed so far is pretty much everything you'd need to know to create and edit the design of scenes in Twitch Studio. For this example, I've covered what you may need in putting together your main scene for people to watch your show.

As detailed earlier, I would suggest you make additional scenes, such as a pre-show scene and interval scene. I have detailed what components these scenes should have in the section about designing a show in OBS. Get ideas for what to include from there, but add elements using the Twitch Studio software.

Using your webcam directly in Twitch Studio

The instructions I've given in this guide are based around importing a video call from Zoom, or another video meeting software. This will allow you to have multiple participants in the show at one time. If you are doing a one person show, you could skip using a video meeting software and just add you webcam and mic as layers in Twitch Studio.

To add the webcam click add layer and choose your webcam.

To add your mic, look to the bottom left of Twitch Studio and you'll see controls for both your camera to be switched on/off, and the audio mixer. Here you can click to add an audio input device, adjust volume, and mute your mic/desktop audio during the shows.

X: DESIGNING YOUR SHOW IN XSPLIT BROADCASTER

Once you have launched the XSplit Broadcaster software, you'll be met with a preview window in the centre of the screen, and a list sources and scenes below.

Adding your video meeting

The first thing we'll do is add a video call into the show we're building. For this example, we'll use Zoom. At the bottom left of the screen, click on 'add source' and then from the menu choose 'Desktop capture' and select Zoom Meeting.

The Zoom meeting will display and will likely appear one quarter the size of the preview window. To resize it, you can hover your mouse cursor over the edge of the element you've added and drag it to the right size. Alternatively, right click and from the menu that pops up choose layout and change the width and height of the Zoom window.

You can also check the box to lock the position.

Adjusting elements with filters and effects

If you right click any element you've added, you'll see a menu with tabs for colour, layout and effects. Playing with these can allow you to add effects to your video call (or any element you've added). Here's a few things that I felt may enhance your show.

Chroma key

If you want to remove a colour for a greenscreen style effect, you can do so with the chroma key tool. This allows you to pick any colour from the screen and remove it. This will make the area that had the colour transparent. Later when we talk about adding video overlays, you'll need to use the chroma key tool on your premade video elements. This will allow your video meeting to be seen from under the overlay.

3D transform

You can create a similar effect of a video being displayed at an angle like you often see on news programs or on instant replays in sports shows. To do this, right click the video element and under layout you will see 2D/3D transform. Change the values under the X, Y and Z boxes to change the angle of the video.

You can also achieve this by holding the shift key and clicking and dragging the element with your mouse.

Filters

Under the effects tab you'll see that you can add a variety of effects that change up the look of the element. These range from giving the element a pixelated look, inverting the colours and more.

The effects tab also give you the option to add masking to the element, so you could change the shape of the video meeting if you wanted. This would allow for more complex cropping than would be available from just using the cropping tool.

Adding a logo/other picture elements

Click add source and then image file. Pick the image you want to add as a logo. GIF/PNG elements allow for transparent backgrounds, so keep this in mind when designing your logos. You can then drag and resize the logo with your mouse.

Adding a video overlay

Click add source and then video file. From here pick the video file you wish to add from your hard drive.

To ensure any video overlay plays on loop, right click the video and under the media tab, where it says 'Play' choose the forever option and the video will loop.

Note that a video overlay will sit on top of your video meeting, and unless you just want a small element like a timer or animated logo in one corner, the video will completely obscure the video meeting at full size. As you cannot have transparent elements in videos, make sure any areas you would want to see through are a single colour (such as green) and use the chroma key effect as described earlier to remove the colour. With this done, you'll now be able to have video elements overlaying your video meeting.

Lower thirds

A 'lower third' is the name for the onscreen graphics you'll often see on news, sports and documentaries that may say a person's name, location or other pieces of information. XSplit gives you the option to add these as a source and has a variety of templates to work with.

You can also apply all the same filters to the lower third as you can other elements, so you can easily change the look, size and add transitions to make them appear/disappear with fades and such like.

Camera

If you want to do a solo show, you don't have to use a separate video meeting software such as Zoom or Skype and you could just import your webcam view.

Whiteboard

If you'd like to draw on the screen during your virtual theatre show, you can add a whiteboard which will allow the person running the stream to easily draw on top of the view of the show. This feature can be used in a variety of creative ways to enhance a show, although if others are in the show via something like Zoom, they would not be able to see what is being drawn unless they watched the live stream of your show.

Audio files

If you want to add some background music or sound effects, you can add these into the design of your show and activate/deactivate them from the list of sources by clicking the eye icon.

Once added, you'll be able to right click the name of the audio file to access the controls for it under the media tab of the pop-up menu. You can also change the audio output to be out loud on your computer's speakers, or just for the audience to hear through the stream. If you play it out loud, the audio will be picked up by your microphone and may sound poorer quality.

Additional scenes

The bottom right side of the screen will show a list of all your scenes. As in my guides to other software in this book, I would recommend you have separate scenes for the pre-show, interval/be right back, end of show and technical difficulties.

The process of designing each additional scene is the same as described for your main/live show scene.

Web Pages

You can integrate a webpage into your stream. Click add source and choose web page and type in the web address for the site you want to integrate into your show. Unlike some other broadcasting software and services, this web page integration allows you to interact with the website from within the preview of your show in XSplit. This is superior to rival ways of screensharing as they usually only allow you to view a webpage and not scroll or navigate through them.

Screensharing

If you'd like to screenshare anything from your computer, such as an open programme, or your desktop, click add source and choose desktop capture and then the name of your monitor display or open application to display it in the stream.

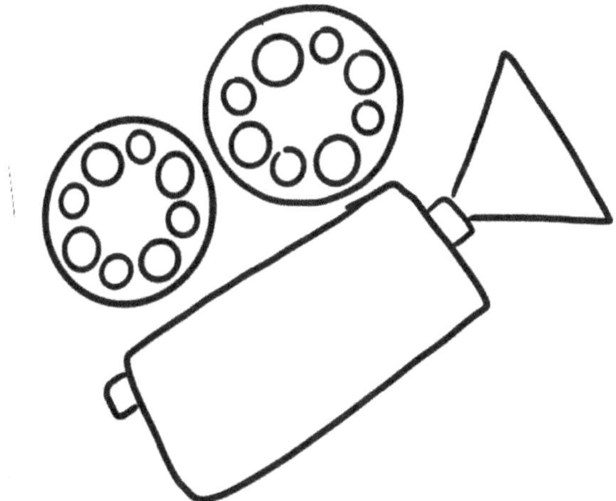

XI: DESIGNING YOUR SHOW WITH DISCORD AND THE DISCORD COMPUTER APP

Note: Before we continue how to design your show using Discord, at the time of writing the Discord computer app will only broadcast to Discord itself. Discord also works differently to other video meeting software in this list, in that when you join the server channel with your video on, anyone who is also a member of that server will be able to join you or see you. You can set channel permissions if you want to restrict access.

For creating a virtual theatre show, it may be better to use a private server on Discord and just see Discord as the video meeting space for you and your team. You could then screenshare the call from Discord into another broadcasting software such as OBS to broadcast it to other social media channels.

Getting started

Once you're signed up to Discord and have installed the computer app, launch the programme.

On the left hand of the display, you'll see a list of any servers you are connected to. Servers are used to connect with others, and you can either have private or public servers. For this example, we'll assume you already have a server (click the + symbol to create one if not).

Now, at the bottom left side of the screen, you'll see the options to turn on your camera or screenshare. Click this and select your camera if one isn't connected. You should also be presented with the option to invite others to join you. Click invite and either invite a friend from your connections or click copy to get an invite link.

As with other guides in this book, I would suggest you have at least two webcams visible on screen whilst designing your shows so you get a sense of what the controls are and where the positioning of things will be.

Virtual backgrounds

Users can add their own virtual backgrounds. Click the arrow next to the webcam icon from the bottom centre of the screen and you'll see the option to change video background. You will be presented with a selection of videos that you can add as a virtual background in your webcam view, or you can choose to blur your actual background or just leave it visible.

It does give the option for custom virtual backgrounds, but these are for subscribers to their Nitro plan only.

Layout

You can switch between grid view to see everyone in the video meeting at once, or choose focus mode, which will spotlight one person in a larger window. The other participants will appear in smaller windows along the bottom of the screen, and you can click on them to put them in focus.

Screensharing

Click the screenshare icon from the left panel and it will give you a list of displays or application windows to choose to display. Once you have selected the source you wish to share click go live and the window will be shared as an additional window in the stream view.

Note that clicking go live is to only go live with the screen/window you are sharing, and that if you are in the server/channel with your webcam on, you are already live and viewable to anyone able to see that channel in the server.

Using Discord in other broadcasting software

If you want to use discord as a video meeting place, but also want to broadcast out to other social channels, you'll need to use another broadcasting software at the same time as Discord.

Launch whatever other broadcasting software you wish to use and click to add a source or screenshare. Now select the Discord window, or display the screen that Discord is visible on and you'll be able to add the Discord meeting into your preferred broadcasting software.

You will now be free to add overlays, chat boxes, and other features that you cannot do natively in Discord to the design of your show.

XII: DESIGNING YOUR SHOW IN OMLET ARCADE

Omlet Arcade is a smart device app and is perhaps most useful for virtual theatre for its ability to stream to multiple social platforms at once from a mobile/tablet.

Design wise, there are very limited things you can do directly in Omlet Arcade. It's screenshare functionality will allow you to stream the video feed from other applications, which can be useful for virtual theatre. This would allow you to create solo performer shows using Snap Chat filters, or other similar apps. You could also use it to screenshare Zoom or Microsoft Teams meetings to have multiple participants and design elements like virtual backgrounds.

The app also allows you to stream directly from the app using your device's camera. This again, could be useful for creating solo shows, so let's take a look at anything you can do to customise the design in Omlet Arcade itself.

Custom design elements

Once the app is launched, tap the centre button with a plus symbol at the bottom of the screen. This will bring up the creation tools. There is a video editor, which you may find useful for editing clips, and a screen record function, but to create a live virtual theatre show, tap go live.

This will bring up the options of what you are streaming and where you plan to stream to. We'll revisit this menu in the setting up your stream to go live section, but for a design purpose, let's explore the two main options for types of content.

Streaming a game/Screenshare

The top options on the stream page are to stream a game or to stream real life. Even though it says 'Game' what this will actually stream is whatever you have displayed on your smart device screen at the time. This can be handy for streaming from applications like Zoom, Skype, Snap Chat etc as they all give more options for what can be achieved design wise than Omlet Arcade's Real Life option.

Real Life

If you select the real life option you will stream out a view from your device's built in camera.

Orientation

Once you've selected your stream type, you'll be presented with the settings menu. If you tap on stream settings, you'll be able to change the orientation of the stream between portrait and landscape.

Overlays

From the settings menu after you have chosen your stream type, you will have the opportunity to add an overlay. There are a few that you can choose from, or you can choose to customise one yourself. Customisation only goes as far as allowing you to choose a picture from your device to use like a profile picture and to add a text message to the bottom of the screen.

Other onscreen elements

Whether you stream a video game or real life, you can choose to add a custom onscreen watermark, as well as custom thumbnail and shield mode image.

Shield mode allows you to place an overlay onto your stream so that if you need to log in to an account or input other sensitive information into an application, the viewers wouldn't see what you are typing.

XIII: DESIGNING YOUR STREAM IN STREAM LABS MOBILE APP

Getting Started

Once the app is launched, tap the menu icon in the top left corner of the screen. If you haven't done so, you'll need to connect the app to one of the available social media platforms that you may want to stream to. This is as simple as clicking connect and following onscreen instructions to give permission for the app to connect.

Adding layers

From the menu click editor. You could choose to have a premade layer, but we'll do things manually. Pick the layers option and then click the + symbol. The first thing we'll add is an overlay, so pick 'add a Stream Labs graphic' and choose one of the available graphics to add to your show design.

Once added, you'll be able to drag the graphic to whatever position is useful and drag the corners to resize it. Tapping the three-dot menu icon on the element will bring up several options. This includes the ability to rotate the graphic, or lock its position and scaling. This is useful so you don't accidentally move it once you have it in place where you want it.

Adding custom graphics and logos

If you want to add a custom overlay or logo, tap layers and the plus symbol, and choose the add custom item option. Now select upload image from device and you'll be able to add any graphics you may have designed such as custom overlays and logos.

Adding custom text

If you want to add on screen text, tap layers and then the plus symbol and select add custom item, followed by add custom text. Now you can type in whatever you want, change the font and the font size.

Widgets

You can add widgets from the layers menu. Widgets include spin wheels which are useful for selecting random words or names. This could be useful in a virtual theatre show if there is a randomised element, or a competition where you want to pick a name of a winner at random.

You can also add a variety of other widgets such as a viewer count, tip jar and sponsor banner.

Themes

You can add themes from a selection available from Stream Labs. This feature is available only for Stream Labs Prime subscribers. If you can afford it and don't wish to source or create your own onscreen graphics this can be an easy way to add some style to your show.

Adding your camera or video meeting into the Stream Labs mobile app

Note: The following information will be duplicated in both this section and the setting up your stream to go live sections of this book. A single method will achieve both goals to add your camera/video call in a design sense, and also allow you to start streaming.

Using Stream Labs mobile app gives you the option to either add your device's camera as a layer, or to screen capture your use of other apps into the stream.

When the app starts, you should get the option to allow access to your camera and mic. When you go live with your camera visible, this is a suitable setup for a one person show or podcast.

If you want to stream a multi person show, it's possible to screen record a video call from software like the Zoom app (which we'll use as the example here).

To set this up, make sure your camera is switched off in the Stream Labs app, and open Zoom. Once yourself and any fellow performers are in the meeting and ready to go live, head back over to the Stream Labs app. Tap the menu icon and choose screen capture. It'll ask you which destination/s you want to stream to, and if you'd like to name the show and then you can go live.

Once you've pressed to go live, just go back into the Zoom app and the audience will be able to see the Zoom meeting being streamed live.

14: OPTIMIZING YOUR SHOW FOR A STABLE PERFORMANCE

Before you go live, you should consider what quality you intend to stream at. This will depend on three main factors:

Factor 1: How fast your internet is.

The faster your internet connection is, the better it will cope with a higher quality stream.

Factor 2: How powerful your computer is

If your internet is slow, a powerful computer will only help so much, but a weak computer will struggle with more advanced streams before the internet even factors into the equation. If your computer is powerful, you'll be able to aim for a higher quality stream.

Factor 3: How advanced your stream is

If your show is very simple, without many layers or filters, there is a good chance you'll be OK with a lesser computer and regular internet connection. If you add more and more to your virtual theatre show, you will find that the computer and internet has more data to handle and things can start to crash.

How to avoid issues

An easy mistake to make when you first start streaming is to overlook setting up the quality of your stream to be something that is manageable by your computer and within the limits of your internet connection. Here are some tips to get a smooth stream.

Reduce resolution of images and videos

If you have print quality images and Ultra HD videos as layers in your stream, they will take more resources to stream. See if you can reduce their resolution and file size.

Unload files when they're not in use

Some programmes such as OBS will offer for you to tick a box to unload a file when it's not being displayed. This can take some strain off your computer. A downside is that reloading a image/video again may mean it appears after a very short delay, but I've never experienced this be more than a second or two.

Change quality and frame rate in your video settings

If you are using software like Zoom for your video call, you can select to turn your camera to HD quality or not. If your stream is struggling, consider switching it off from high definition.

Change the quality of your stream output

If you're streaming directly to a social media platform, or streaming directly from Zoom or StreamYard, you may see some limited options about your stream quality. Usually these will be limited to asking if you wish to stream in HD or not, and sometimes it may ask what framerate you wish to use.

720 is still HD, but 1080 is full HD. 4K is becoming more common at the time of writing but is far from the typical standard as yet.

Framerate wise, I would suggest you don't do more than 30 frames per second (fps). If you enjoy streaming video games, it may be more relevant to stream at 60 fps, but for virtual theatre 30 fps is more than suitable.

Bitrate and more advanced settings

If you are using a more customisable solution to broadcast your shows, such as OBS, Twitch Studio or Stream Labs, you may have a greater selection of options for stream quality. This may include options to change the resolution, frames per second and bitrate.

Whichever software you are using, head into the settings menu. Here you may find the option to resize the stream's base canvas resolution and output resolution. The higher the resolution, the more data your computer and internet connection have to deal with, so you may want to consider if you wish to use 4K, Full HD, or lower resolutions.

Also in settings, you will find the Frames Per Second (FPS) values. Again, I should imagine that 30 frames per second will be sufficient for most virtual theatre needs, and 60 FPS if you were streaming a video game.

In software such as OBS or Stream Labs, there will be an output section in the settings, and here you will see options for streaming and recording. This is worth noting, as you could have different standards of quality settings depending on if you want to stream live or just record to your computer.

The recording options are simply there for if you wish to record your show, and don't want to broadcast it live. It is the streaming section that is more important for what we're focusing on.

Under video bitrate you can change the value, and this will dictate how much information is being streamed out. At the time of writing, I usually stream out between 3500 Kbps and 4500 Kbps. As technology improves, you may find that your computer/internet can easily handle this and want to up it further. If you need to reduce it to help your system cope, then that is ok too.

15: SETTING UP YOUR STREAM TO GO LIVE

Now that all the design elements are in place, you are ready to test everything and go live. I would still recommend you look at the tips for the cast and technician later in the book before you rush into a full show, but it's OK at this stage to do a test run to make sure everything is working.

Going live directly on a social media platform

I won't talk you through step by step of every platform, just because social media platforms continually update their design and how things work. Instead, here is a general overview of what to expect.

Going live on mobile/Smart device

There will usually be a button to 'Go Live' within the social media app. Press it, and you should get the option to go live immediately. There may be a few options to invite a friend to join the stream, or add filters, but other than that it's that simple.

Do note that going live like this from a smart device will mean you are very limited in what you can do on your stream compared to if you use streaming software on a computer.

Going live from broadcasting software on your computer

To start streaming your show live using broadcasting software from your computer you may need a stream key. As detailed earlier, a stream key is a unique code, which you will get from a social media platform, or aggregate streaming service, and is used to connect your broadcasting software to your social channels.

How to find your stream key

To find your stream key from a single platform (such as Facebook, or YouTube) you need to go onto that platform's website and click to create a stream or go live. From there you'll be given the option to go live immediately with a webcam or use broadcasting software. If you choose the latter, you should be given a stream key code. Once you've found it, copy it to the clipboard.

Once you have the stream key code you'll need to paste it into where you input stream keys on your broadcasting software. Usually this can be found in the broadcasting software's settings, but we'll detail how it works for some of the platforms as we continue.

Going live directly from Zoom

Once in the Zoom meeting, click the three-dot menu and choose to go live on your preferred social media platform. It may ask you to log in to authorise your live stream and also to name it. Once done, you will then go live on that platform.

Going live directly from Skype, Google Meet, Facebook Messenger Rooms and Microsoft Teams

At the time of writing, there is not currently a way to go live directly from Skype, Google Meet, Facebook Messenger Rooms or Microsoft Teams. If you wish to use any of these programmes as your video conferencing software, you will need to import the view of the meeting into broadcasting software such as OBS.

OBS/SLOBS

Once you have a stream key copied to the clipboard, open up OBS/Stream Labs OBS and go into settings (this may be represented by a cog wheel icon) and choose the 'stream' subcategory. It may ask you to pick what platform you are planning to stream to, and it will ask you for your stream key.

Paste in the stream key and click OK. Now you will be able to click go live/start streaming and your show will begin broadcasting live on your social media platform of choice.

StreamYard

Once you're logged in on the StreamYard website, choose destinations and then 'add a destination' to add as many social media platforms from the options that you'd like. You'll be asked to connect and authorise that StreamYard can post to these sites, so connect any accounts you'd like to stream to.

Once this is set up, click on 'broadcast' to create a live broadcast. At this stage it will ask you to choose which destinations you wish to broadcast to, and you'll be able to select as many as your subscription level allows you to broadcast to at any one time.

Once selected, fill out the requested info for your broadcast. This will differ slightly depending which platforms you plan to stream to but will include the name and description of your stream.

Once created you'll be able to enter the studio. Once in the studio, you will see the 'go live' button in the corner of the screen. Press this and you will go live instantly to your selected platforms.

Twitch Studio

Once you've launched Twitch Studio, logged in to your Twitch account and set up your stream, going live is as simple as clicking start steam from just underneath the stream preview window.

As noted elsewhere, Twitch Studio will only stream to the Twitch platform, and not to other social media sites like Facebook or YouTube.

You won't need a stream key from Twitch to go live, as you'll have logged in to Twitch Studio with your Twitch account. This automatically readies the software to stream to your channel.

Multi-streaming to other broadcasting software with Restream

There are a few ways to stream to multiple platforms at once. If you wish to do this, instead of getting a stream key from a specific platform such as Twitch or Facebook, you will get a stream key from the Restream.io website.

When you create a Restream account, you'll be able to connect to multiple social media platforms to stream to.

You will then be presented with your stream key, and once copied, you paste it into your broadcasting software just as you would if you streamed to only one platform.

Multi-streaming with Restream Studio

Once you are logged in to Restream and enter Restream Studio, you will see the name of your show at the top of the screen above the preview window. You can click on it to update the name of your show if required.

Next to this is the destination selection tool. Click on it and you'll be able to toggle on/off any social media platforms that you have connected and would like to stream to. Once these are selected just click the go live button to the top right of the stream preview window and you're done.

XSplit Broadcaster

Once your stream is designed and ready to go live, click the stream button at the top centre of the screen to set up where you will stream to.

You'll be presented with a list of all the available services that you can connect to via XSplit. Depending on the service/social media platform you wish to connect to, you will need to log in or authorise your account to link to XSplit.

Once this is connected, you'll also see options to customise the quality of the stream, including which video codec and video and audio bitrate you wish to use. At the time of writing, the standard that came up is the x264 codec, and 2400 kbps for the video bitrate. The latter certainly can be increased for a better-quality image, but this is an area which will depend on your computer/internet speed and will be able to be increased as technology improves.

Once you have this set up, click ok, and then hit the stream button to connect to your chosen platform. You may have to fill in details of the title of the show, genre etc and then can go live.

Omlet Arcade

Before you begin

As you will be streaming the activity on your smart device's screen, you should make sure you switch your device to 'do not disturb' or switch off notifications so that text/private messages, or other notifications aren't broadcast live on your stream.

You may also want to have any applications such as Zoom, Skype or other applications you plan to broadcast set up and ready to go before you start your stream. Otherwise the audience will see you setting up the other apps.

Setting up the stream

Once you are logged in to your Omlet Arcade account on your smart device, tap the + symbol and choose go live.

Firstly, you'll have to choose between screensharing your device by selecting 'Game' or streaming from your device's camera by selecting 'Real life'.

After this you'll see a list of the available platforms that you can stream to. If you have a free account, you can only stream to one social media platform at a time, but if you have a subscription you can select multiple destinations to stream to at once. Platforms supported include Omlet Arcade itself, Facebook, YouTube, Twitch and Nimo TV.

Once selected tap next and you'll have additional settings you can adjust if you want. Once you're ready tap done followed by start to begin the stream.

Stream Labs Mobile App

Note: The following information will be duplicated in both the 'designing your show' chapter and this chapter of this book. A single method will achieve both goals to add your camera/video call in a design sense, and also allow you to start streaming.

Using Stream Labs mobile app gives you the option to either add your device's camera as a layer, or to screen capture your use of other mobile apps into the stream.

When the app starts, you should get the option to allow access to your camera and mic. When you go live with your camera visible, this is a suitable setup for a one person show or podcast.

If you want to stream a multi person show, it's possible to screen record a video call from software like the Zoom app (which we'll use as the example here).

To set this up, make sure your camera is switched off in the Stream Labs app, and open Zoom. Once you and any fellow performers are in the meeting and ready to go live, head back over to the Stream Labs app. Tap the menu icon and choose screen capture. It'll ask you which destination/s you want to stream to, and also if you want to name the show. Once done you can go live.

Once you've pressed to go live, just go back into the Zoom app and the audience will be able to see the Zoom meeting being streamed live.

16: SOCIAL MEDIA PLATFORMS AND THEIR BENEFITS/DIFFERENCES

There are many social media platforms where you could stream your live virtual theatre show to, and all of them have their unique features and presentation. You'll almost certainly have personal experience with one or more of these platforms, but here is an overview to the platforms and some thoughts as to why each one may or may not be the right fit for you, your company and your show.

Keep in mind that social media platforms are constantly evolving and new ones are emerging, whilst old ones disappear. In the time since I started broadcasting Extreme Improv Xstreamed shows, I've seen major platforms such as Mixer and Periscope cease to exist, and seen the likes of TikTok rise in popularity.

Platforms also take inspiration from each other, and so unique features of one platform may well be integrated into others in the future. As examples, many platforms started to introduce the concept of short 15 second or 60 second videos in response to TikTok, whilst TikTok have allowed for progressively longer videos. This means the unique features of each platform are getting blurred, and you may find that content you create for one platform may be able to be repurposed on many now.

YouTube

For a creator of virtual theatre shows, I would say the main place you should target is YouTube. It allows longform videos and is easy to watch on any device including on televisions.

Most importantly, YouTube is a fairly safe place to store an archive of your past shows. Some platforms do not keep videos of live streams indefinitely, but YouTube does, and it's easy to organise shows into playlists.

YouTube is also a platform which has every kind of content imaginable, including theatre, so there will be an audience for virtual theatre on the platform.

Monetisation can be reached after you gain a certain number of subscribers and viewers have watched a certain number of hours of your videos within a year time period. Whilst not as easy to reach as some monetisation levels on this list, the positive is that people can watch your shows in their own time, and don't have to watch live to help you towards this goal.

Twitch

Twitch is a platform geared primarily towards gamers. Whilst you do get all kinds of content on the platform, such as podcasts, people just chatting with their viewers and art and performance-based content, Twitch is undoubtably best known as a place where people stream video games.

A plus of the platform is that if you stream regularly enough, the criteria for the lowest level of monetisation on the platform is quite low. The next levels up are much trickier to reach unless you have a continual audience, and this audience have to watch your content live to meet this criteria.

Twitch also doesn't keep the archive of your shows online indefinitely, so if you just stream to Twitch, it would be recommended to ensure your shows are recorded in some way. This can be done with software like SLOBS or OBS which allow you to record as you broadcast.

Facebook

The great thing about streaming shows on Facebook is that it is a very easy place to share your live videos. As the platform is much more than just a video site like YouTube or Twitch, you are more likely to have people discover your show from their Facebook newsfeed.

Videos that are shared on Facebook also auto play. This means that as people scroll past it they may see a snippet of what is going and it may catch their attention.

For marketing and discoverability, Facebook groups and pages can also be leveraged to help your shows reach a wider audience and not just be limited to people who already like your page.

A downside of Facebook is that depending on how you have your page set up, you may find that shows are not stored indefinitely. Some settings may allow this, but as a personal note, I once lost many months of archived videos from my Facebook page. This was because I had a page set up as a Gaming Video Creator page, and Facebook changed their policy on archiving videos of this nature.

In terms of monetisation options, Facebook offer many ways to get monetised. For video related ways, the ability to gain audience donations (known as stars on the platform) can be obtained quite quickly, but after this, the next level of criteria to have adverts play in your shows is much more challenging to access.

Twitter

Twitter is a platform designed primarily for short form content. Tweets only allow for short text-based posts, and uploaded videos are usually limited to short clips. After Periscope closed as a platform, Twitter did integrate being able to live stream long shows as a feature.

Twitter videos will stay archived on your account indefinitely, which is an advantage over some others, but doesn't offer a great way to search through and view older videos from a playlist or gallery.

Going live on Twitter is usually done from a smart device, using the device's camera and therefore very limited in terms of what is possible. You can use broadcasting software on a computer to stream to the platform and create shows with higher production values.

Monetisation options are also limited on Twitter, and although there are options to add a tip jar to your profile, monetisation from ads and sponsorships isn't as fleshed out as on other platforms.

TikTok

TikTok is designed as a short form video platform. Most videos last between 15 and 60 seconds, although recent changes allow you to add up to ten-minute-long videos. If you meet certain criteria, you can also live stream to the platform, although like Twitter, this is usually done through a smart device. If you want to stream a fuller show using computer-based broadcasting software this is possible using a service like Restream.

Instagram

Much like Twitter and TikTok described above, you can go live on Instagram, but the platform isn't really designed around this concept. Instead, the platform is primarily for photos with short captions. Video content is increasing in popularity on Instagram, and like Facebook, which is also owned by Meta, there are lots of short videos (known as Reels on Insta).

If you want to stream a computer designed show on Instagram, you'll need to use broadcasting software in conjunction with a service like Restream.

Streaming to another video platform

There are countless video platforms out there including the likes of Dailymotion, DLive, Trovo, Nimo TV, Vimeo or others. Many of them are currently much smaller than the likes of Facebook or YouTube, and as such I've made the decision to focus on the more widely used platforms. Sites such as Dailymotion or Vimeo may feel similar to YouTube in ways whilst Trovo and Dlive may be more reminiscent of Twitch.

Depending on where you are in the world, it may be that your local platform of choice hasn't been featured, so do your best to research as to how they are unique from the likes of YouTube etc. Also see what they offer in terms of archiving your videos online, so you don't lose records of your shows, and whether there are monetisation options for your show to earn.

17: VIRTUAL SHOWS, COPYRIGHT ISSUES AND OTHER LEGAL STUFF

OK, before we get into things here, there's a couple of extremely important things I need to make clear from the start of this chapter.

Number 1: I am not a lawyer, and you shouldn't mistake this as legal advice or take anything I've said as gospel.

And Number 2: Copyright law is a gigantic topic! I could write a whole book on the subject, and that is still despite me not being a lawyer!

Now that's said, allow me to give you some food for thought around the types of things you need to consider so that you don't get yourself into legal trouble with your virtual theatre shows.

Famous music

You can't use famous songs in your shows unless you license it from the copyright holders.

This means you can't play We Will Rock You by Queen, a song by the Beatles or anything else like this that you may have a copy of.

It doesn't matter if you bought a record, cassette, CD, MP3 or any other type of recording of the song. Owning a copy just gives you the right to play and listen to it, and not to use it in your shows.

It doesn't matter if you only want to play 30 seconds of it, or even 5 seconds. If you don't have a license for the song, you can't use any amount of it. A huge myth people believe is that you are ok to use 10 or 30 seconds. You can't. Not without a license.

If you do use it, you are likely to find that your videos will be demonetised on any social media platform, and the video will display adverts which the copyright holders of the song will profit from. Not you!

Imagine if you made a 2-hour virtual theatre show and at the end you play a famous song for 3 minutes. Your entire 2-hour show will be demonetised. This may happen straight away, or it may happen weeks or months later. The point is, if you use something you don't have the rights to use, it becomes a ticking time bomb which could become demonetised at any point.

You may also find that your video is blocked in certain countries if you use certain songs. So you would have less potential audience.

And worst of all, you may find that using something which is someone else's copyright could get you in trouble with or banned from a social media platform. If there is either an automatic or manual copyright claim made against your video, you may find that the video is removed and/or that you have restrictions or strikes placed on your channel. This is a very worrying area to get into with your channel as multiple strikes could see your channel taken off a platform entirely.

You can't beat the system by playing the songs yourself

A mistake people often make is that they believe if they play a famous song on a piano or sing it themselves, that they'll be OK from a copyright standpoint. Those people would be wrong.

Even if you're not using an exact copy of a performance by the copyright holder, they still own the rights to the tune and the lyrics.

Now, you may be thinking to yourself that you've seen loads of people do covers of famous singer's songs. You would be correct, but these people may have been allowed to leave their track up on a platform, but it may be demonetised.

It is true that the software that automatically recognises copyrighted tracks may not instantly recognise your version of a famous song, but like I said before, if you didn't write the tune or lyrics, the people that did could raise a complaint.

Beyond getting in trouble with the social media platforms, a copyright holder may just decide to sue you for copyright theft. This could take the form of someone seeking for you to cease and desist from using their copyrighted material, all the way up to them seeking damages and any other penalties that can be thrown at you by law.

What about videos and images?

Music is maybe the most commonly problematic thing you may want to use in your shows, but copyright issues can come from anything you didn't create. This extends to video clips from movies, TV shows, video game footage, other YouTube videos, photos, clip art and everything in between.

There may be ways in which you can use elements of some of these if the usage is seen as transformative or fair usage. I'll discuss this more a little later on though.

Broadly speaking though, if you are creating a virtual theatre show, you should take caution when using anything you don't own the rights to. If someone else created it, they own the copyright...broadly speaking.

You mentioned video games? Aren't most videos on YouTube just video games?

OK, so this does go slightly off topic from virtual theatre, but since we're here, let's quickly cover it as it will help us understand what we can and can't do.

Most video game companies these days won't kick up much fuss if you share footage of their video games. There are several reasons for this, but the main ones include that because video games are interactive, a video online cannot fully give away the main intended experience of a game, and that is to be able to play it. The other big reason they allow it is because the video of someone playing a game may encourage others to want to play it as well, and therefore it gives the games free advertising.

This is different from music and movies, as playing those online will essentially give the entire intended experience, which is to listen and watch them, away for free.

Despite most gaming companies now allowing players to upload or live stream videos of their games online, there are still times when a games company will hit a video with a copyright claim. You will find that their policies on what they find acceptable to stream or not changes regularly.

Bringing this back to virtual theatre, this doesn't mean you can automatically get away with using video game music in your shows, or that you can produce Super Mario Bros the Musical online. The music, story and characters will all be copyrighted, and at any point a company may decide to raise a complaint.

What about parodies?

OK, let's stick with Super Mario Bros the Musical for a moment. Would you be able to produce this show, using characters you didn't create or video or music you don't own if it is a parody? The answer is maybe, and whether you get away with this or not may depend on how clear the parody is, and how determined the lawyers of the copyright holders are.

A parody may be obviously inspired by another work, but for it to count as a parody, it needs to clearly not be the original It also needs to provide some kind of comedic twist, usually to provide some commentary or observation on the original.

As an example, you can't just take the story of Harry Potter and present it in the exact same way as the original, but name it Larry Dotter. That would be seen as plagiarism. If, however, Larry Dotter was to point out the flaws of the story of Harry Potter and also make references to the real-world actors who plays Harry Potter characters, it would be much more likely to be seen as a parody.

Let's talk fair usage

You may have come across the term fair usage when it comes to video, music, images and such like.

The easiest example of fair usage is if you were to make a documentary. If you are making a documentary about The Beatles, you would be able to use short video clips, music clips, quotes from books, images and such like to illustrate the subject you are making the documentary about.

There is a fine line with fair usage that can easily be crossed, so for example, it wouldn't be fair usage to play an entire music video from a famous band as part of a documentary about them. This would be seen as excessive use.

Fair usage doesn't only count for documentaries, and can also apply for works such as plays, films and of course, virtual theatre. For example, if you were making a project based on someone's life, whether biographical or fictional, it can be seen as reasonable that they may have interacted with something that is in copyright.

If your play or film has a character who is obsessed with Disneyland and wanted to have the character wear a T-shirt, display a poster, or sing a line from Beauty and the Beast, there is a good chance that you would be able to get away with this as fair usage. You may even be able to have a clip of a copyrighted song or video play in the background.

The usage in cases like these will need to be seen as relevant, and not excessive or exploitative of the original copyrighted work.

As a slight warning here, even if you feel that your use of a clip/song is fair usage, it could easily get detected by automated music recognition on platforms like YouTube. So, in this sense, I would still suggest you avoid using things that can easily run you into issues. A documentary is different as this will be more obvious to argue as fair usage if a claim arises.

Defamation

To give another example, many within the performing arts profession will have come across the idea that clothes you wear for stage or screen shouldn't show any brands or logos on. Likewise, a company making a project may want to avoid showing specific brands such as Coca Cola, Pepsi etc. Using these could be seen as copyright violations, or break a company's policy on product placement or sponsorship.

This doesn't mean you can't use them, as it is reasonable that a person has to wear clothes or eat/drink and if these products are created for these uses it would be fair that you use them in your show.

Their inclusion may ask for issues though. One kind of issue you may not expect is that a copyright holder may say your use of their copyrighted product is defamatory or damaging to their brand. If, for example, you had a character who said one brand of cola was great and the other is filled with pond water, this could creep into defamation. Another example may be that if you have a character wear a branded T-shirt and they always wear it when they commit bank robbery or murder, the company could claim that you are creating an association between their brand and violent crimes. They could claim this damages the good image of their brand.

Public domain works

One type of content you are allowed to use to your heart's content are public domain works. Broadly speaking, public domain works are usually works that are older things where the copyright has run out, or newer things, where the copyright holder has given permission for their work to enter the public domain. You usually will require some evidence that this is the case if it should later be disputed.

How long copyright lasts before it expires varies from country to country and is continually evolving. At the time of writing, copyright lasts until death plus 70 years in the UK. This means if someone owns a copyright, they can own it until they die, and then a countdown of 70 years will begin. At the end of this 70-year period, the work will enter the public domain.

One thing to be aware of, is that just because one work is in the public domain, it doesn't mean another is.

For example, if a film was made in 1930, and the director was the copyright holder, and they died in 1931, the film would go into the public domain in 2001. If, however, the film contained a performance or recording of a song by a well-known singer, who independently owned the copyright of the song they sang, and they lived until 1971, the song wouldn't enter the public domain until 2041.

This doesn't mean that you cannot use the film in it's entirely or portions of it until 2041. If the estate of the singer wanted to raise a complaint if they felt you were exploiting the song for gain as a stand-alone work, they could do this. I can't say how things would turn out based on this hypothetical situation, but it's something to keep in mind and do your own research on.

Creative commons licenses

Something I can only speak vaguely on, are what are known as creative commons licences. This is a large topic which I can put my hands up and say, 'I don't fully understand, and I'm not going to do all the research required to be able to write a few competent paragraphs for this book!'. There, I said it…better to be honest than me just blagging it.

What I can say is that my understanding is (and hopefully this will help give you the first step to understanding it) that you generally can use things with creative commons licenses, but there may be a few caveats.

For example, there are some creative commons licenses which allow you to use the image, audio, video etc, but that you have to credit the original creator. If you don't, they could raise a complaint.

Another license may allow you to use, and alter the original work, but that you cannot profit from it, or use it commercially. There are several different types of these creative commons licenses, and the best advice I can give is to check the license of anything you plan to use. If you see it has a creative commons license attached, check which one it is and research what it means.

Royalty-free licenses

A royalty-free license isn't the same as public domain or other copyright free licenses. A misconception people have is that if they get a copy of a royalty-free track or video, that they are then free to use it however they want. This is incorrect.

A royalty-free license is a license you obtain form a copyright holder, and usually have to pay for. Once you have the license, you are then free to use the audio/video/image as many times as you like without having to pay repeated royalties.

Once you have the license, you may find that you have to continually prove that you have the rights to use it, and this can be a pain, so keep track of any royalty-free works you are in possession of.

Don't let other people cause you copyright issues by them using things you wouldn't

Sticking with the subject of royalty-free music for a moment, what do you do if you have a guest show or act on your virtual theatre production and they use royalty-free music they own a license to, but you do not?

This is an excellent question, and the best advice I can give would be that you check with any performers what their plans are before they work with you. If they intend to use any music, don't be afraid to say they cannot use something if it is in copyright, or that you don't personally have a license to be able to use it.

Even if they have a license, if you do not, I wouldn't let them use it. Imagine if they said they had a license and lied, or were unhelpful and didn't prove that they could use the music if you were later in a dispute.

You don't want to find yourself in legal disputes, demonetised, or risk losing social media channels because other people haven't done their research.

It may even be worse, and that they intend to play famous songs which will cause you issues. They may not have any ill intent with their plans to use these songs, but to protect the hard work you put into your channel, I would strongly advise that you be clear that certain things cannot be used if they will potentially cause issues.

Do you have the rights to use someone's image?

This is another big topic, but let's go over a few points to help guide you in the right direction. Once again, here I will point out that I'm not a lawyer, and my understanding is based off me being in the UK, and what I believe to be correct. Use this as a starting point, but please do your own research.

If you are filming in a public place, such as on the streets or in a park, you are free to film anything. I'm sure this doesn't mean you can stand outside someone's window and film into their house, and I'm certain there are rules about filming if children are present.

Do remember that social media platforms will now actively ask you if a video is for children, or features children, and your answer may affect the status of the video and its discoverability. Regardless of government laws, each social media platform will have its own policies to protect people.

What being allowed to film in public does mean is that if you do a virtual theatre show where a performer is outside, it's no worries if someone walks past in the background. As long as you don't intentionally make someone the focus of your filming, they should have no complaint if they happen by in the background.

What if someone appears on your show?

If someone has actively and willingly taken part in your virtual theatre show, stage show, film, etc etc, you will have the right to use the footage they appear in. A concern that may arise for virtual theatre producers is that they could receive a request for an old show or footage to be taken down if a performer no longer wants to be featured or associated with that performance.

The resolution of this type of concern will largely depend on your relationship with the performer, but generally speaking, if it is clear that they willingly took part in the production, you have the right to maintain copyright of the video they were in.

You may be familiar with performers having contracts or release forms that allow the usage of someone's image, but these are not essential. They certainly do give the production company something to point to if there were to be concerns later, and they can also be useful to ensure certain promises are kept to the performer as well.

It should be noted that the footage from the virtual theatre show will belong to the producer of the show, and individual performers may request copies of shows, or to be able to use clips to promote themselves. A good producer should have no issue allowing a performer to use clips to promote themselves, but you should be clear on what you are giving permission for them to use.

If they were to download and reupload the entire show on their channel it would compete with and damage the success of your own production. If there is a scene or clip that gives away huge spoilers to the plot, you could also say that you don't want that shared.

If a performer, or anyone else uses a clip within the realm of fair use, that is something you should accept. However, if there is a dispute, the two parties would have to raise why it is or isn't fair usage. In the early stages of a dispute, a social media platform may make a decision based on the complaint or counter presented to them. If this isn't satisfactory for one party, they would be within their right to take things further through a court.

A note I would give to producers is to make sure the context you use any footage of a performer in remains true to the context they agreed to take part in. If you produce a highlights video and show a performer who hasn't worked with you in 10 years, that performer could rightly complain that their inclusion is misleading to their involvement. If the theme of the video makes it clear that their inclusion is to show the history and legacy of your projects, you should be fine.

Likewise, sharing clips of performers out of context could lead to misunderstandings that their performance of a character reflects who they are in real life. If this is the case, they may fairly feel displeased with its usage.

One thing to remember is you can't beat "The Man"

The last thing I'll raise on the topic of legal considerations is that, however fair or unfair certain things may seem, if you are an independent producer, you are unlikely to get very far if you face issues with large organisations.

If you get a copyright complaint from a big company such as a movie studio, a record label or if a social media platform is demonetising or restricting your content, really question if it is worth fighting.

I don't say this to be discouraging or defeatist, and if you require support of any kind, I would always say to seek it out. This includes legal support for the kinds of topics discussed in this chapter, or if you need the support of friends or family if any such stresses seem challenging or overwhelming.

I give the warning that you are unlikely to get far with issues with big organisations, so you don't put in time and energy into something long and drawn out, or negative and destructive. Consider if it is worth fighting, and if that energy is better saved for creative endeavours.

I say this from personal experience of finding videos I have made are limited or taken down when I have been certain I have stayed within the rules of a social media platform and stayed within the law. It can be frustrating, but when exploring how to challenge such issues I found it would have been a mountain to climb. And for what? So one video can be reinstated?

Maybe I was wrong. Like I said I'm not a lawyer.

If there's a music track that causes an issue, try to show you have a license. If there are still issues, get another track. There are millions out there.

If a video clip is someone else's copyright, see if you can cut it out and reupload the video without the disputed clip.

If someone doesn't want to be seen in a video anymore, see if you can cut them out. If not, and you have the right to use it, then apologise that they're not happy but decline to remove it and leave it up.

18: MARKETING YOUR VIRTUAL THEATRE SHOW TO BUILD AN AUDIENCE AND COMMUNITY

We've covered all the equipment and software you'll need to create a virtual theatre show. We've also covered, how to design a show in that software and go live on the internet. Now it's time to cover one of the most challenging aspects of producing a virtual theatre show – getting an audience.

This is a huge subject to cover, so I'm going to make sure we cover the essentials and set you on the right path for success.

Build a community

The best marketing tip I can give you is to build a community around your show and/or company. I know that sounds obvious, but it isn't. So many shows get streamed where the creators have no idea who has watched, without interacting with the audience and if you carry on this way, you will be effectively starting from scratch to get an audience with every performance.

Take the time and show an interest in learning who your audience is. Ask who is interested in your show, and when you find some take note of their age, where they're from, their background and their interests. Getting a sense of this is the most powerful thing you can do to build an audience.

Once you know who has made an effort to watch your show the first time, thank them by interacting with them. Thank them for watching. Tell them you hope to see them again at the next show and chat with them. Building a relationship with the audience can take time, but what you'll find is that once you have a few audience members who feel invested in your show and what you do, they will help spread the word to their friends and circle and that will encourage more people to watch and join the community.

This is the principal of going viral. You start the conversation with a small audience, and they will continue it to the next batch of people, who will continue it to the next batch of people after them. Quickly you'll find it's not just up to you to keep the conversation alive. That isn't to say that you should stop taking part, but you will have to circulate more to interact with larger numbers of people as new people come into the community.

Don't forget those who helped you get where you are

A mistake people often make is that once a few more people join a community, the theatre makers rush to make the new faces feel welcome, which is a good thing, but do it at the expense of neglecting or alienating their original fanbase. Don't do that. Your original fan base is who helped you grow in the early days, and if you continue to make them feel appreciated, they will always be there for you.

Also, you will have had a closer interaction with the original fans because there was only a few of them to interact with. You can feel safe in giving them a little more attention than you may give to newer faces. You can't always give as much time to interact with newer faces, so the newer members of the community won't feel they are neglected, as they never had a greater level of interaction than they do now. This isn't short-changing them either, as your original fan base who are most loyal will help integrate new faces and share the load of community building.

By the time you have fifth, sixth and seventh generation community members you'll find the community is self-sustaining, and you will only have to do maintenance rather than building from scratch each time.

The most loyal and reliable audience and community members

If you want to build a community, you need the first few people to get the ball rolling. These are likely to be friends and family, which is fine for a short while, but you will quickly need to get people outside of your pre-established circle.

A few supportive faces to give comments and share links are great to spread the word, and if you have an important show, the chances are that your friends and family will often be willing to be there for you. This said, don't forget that first and foremost, your friends and family are your friends and family. They're not there to be used, or to just be audience. Don't take them for granted or push them to watch every show as this can add strain if done too much.

Your friends and family can certainly get the ball rolling, but we'll need more tricks up our sleeve to grow beyond our friends list on Facebook.

Create social media pages and a website for your show

If you're serious about people discovering your show and your work overall, you need to make it so that people can find you. You may want to create some or all the following:

Facebook page: A page for your company or show is a great way for people to discover it. You can use it to add regular posts or events that are both fun to engage with and are informative about your show. Most importantly Facebook is a great platform to stream your show to, as it has great sharing functions so you and others can get the word out.

Facebook group: A Facebook group is useful in addition to, or as an alternative to a Facebook page as they feel more focussed on the community. Posts can be more off-topic compared to the more official or business centric posts that are best suited for a Facebook page.

Trusted group members can also be given admin or moderator roles, which help give a sense of the individuals involved in the community.

Twitter: Twitter is great for sharing content as it can quickly spread between users that aren't even connected to one another.

Instagram: Great for photos and videos. A picture can speak a thousand words, so having some eye-catching promo images can be a great conversation starter to get some buzz around your show.

TikTok: Great for sharing informal video updates on your projects, clips from shows, or even specific content made for TikTok which can be great to help reach a wider audience.

Video platforms: YouTube, and Twitch are the main ones I'd say you should create accounts for, but there are dozens more. These two, in addition to Facebook and Twitter are the main targets I'd suggest for live streaming your shows to. You should also consider creating show trailers and channel trailers which can be shared across all social platforms to drum up interest in the shows.

Also, the comments sections on your and other people's videos are a great way to connect to audiences and build a community.

Advertise your show through social media for free

As well as sharing news about your shows and the live streams as posts on your own social media pages, I'd suggest you interact with other individuals, pages, and groups to share your show.

There are Facebook groups for every interest, so if you look up and join groups you haven't created, it is a good way to share news and videos of your show to reach new potential audience members.

Tagging people/other accounts who may have an interest in your projects is a useful way to reach out to specific people/companies. They'll get a notification and be able to directly see what you'd like to show them. When commenting, you can usually put an @ symbol followed by the person's username to tag them. If they take an interest in what you share with them, they may share it to their network of connections. This can be done on all the mentioned platforms.

Don't be annoying though!

Something many people are guilty of is tagging people constantly, or spamming posts to groups. This doesn't usually go over well, and some people will let you know it. Even if people don't let you know it, they may find it annoying and just mute or block you and dismiss anything you have to share in the future. Keep this in mind.

You're much more likely to get a positive reaction and engagement from people if you send them less frequent, but personalised messages, and really consider the tone of what you say. If you just tweet a celebrity saying 'retweet me' they are unlikely to. And if you're going to share something to a group, consider writing a custom message to say why it'd be useful for members of that group. Also try interacting with other people's posts in that group to build connections that way.

Connecting with an audience takes time, and there is a learning curve to it. I'm certain I've been guilty of all the above, and through that I've gained a sense of what works and what doesn't work for me.

Paid advertisements through social media

All the major platforms have created ways where you can give them money in exchange for exposure. You should consider the pros and cons of creating paid ads for your projects. Before you pay for adverts, I would suggest learning about your audience from ads that you can share on groups and pages for free and see what the response is.

Consider who your target audience is, and how you can most effectively communicate your show/company/brand to them. This is another huge topic, so do your research, and consider if images are best for you, or if video adverts are. Think about when and how long your ad campaign should last, and what social platforms would help your audience grow the most.

Posters, flyers and other physical materials

OK, so this feels a little odd for a virtual theatre show, and getting physical materials printed can cost a lot. What I'd suggest is that if you want to target a specific geographic location, such as your hometown, and say there is a virtual theatre show coming up, you can do this. You'd be able to leverage yourself as the hometown hero, and as a local interest story, so in this sense physical publicity materials can make sense.

The reason physical materials for an online show feels odd, is because an online show can have a worldwide audience. So why put cost into just a small area? Consider this, and unless you have a good reason to target one area, I'd suggest you stick to online methods.

If, however, you also have in person shows and you are creating flyers for them, it's totally ok to mention on the flyer that people can also see your virtual theatre shows online. It'd be a missed opportunity not to include that information on a physical publicity material.

Word of mouth

We've spoken about community building online, and using Facebook groups and retweets, but actually talking to people in the flesh to build an audience can also be very successful.

If you attend social or work settings in real life, you can let people know about your projects. If they're interested, they may talk about your shows to other people, and spread news via word of mouth. Just as I said earlier about online communication, make sure you're not annoying. If people suspect that you're being fake or only showing an interest in them so they come to your show, they will smell it a mile away. Be modest and show as much interest in their lives as you'd like them to show in yours and you'll get much better results.

Use online shows to build real life shows and vice versa

If you do both virtual theatre and projects on stage, you can use each one to grow the other. If you do a show online, make sure you tell people at the end, or display a graphic if you have live in person shows coming up.

Likewise, if you are on stage in front of a crowd of people, this is an audience who have already been willing to take the time to watch you. So let them know you'll have more shows on the internet. If you are doing a play, it may not feel appropriate to be seen out of character at the end saying, 'please watch me on YouTube', but if you have front of house people on the door, or signs/posters/roller banners that can let people know about your online shows, then take this opportunity.

Cross promote with others

Depending on your show, you may find that you can have guests from other shows or companies take part in your show, and vice versa. This is an opportunity to make an announcement about your show, and people interested in the guest may now learn about and watch your show.

19: MAKING MONEY WITH YOUR VIRTUAL THEATRE SHOW

Making money through virtual theatre isn't the same as making money through in person theatre. With traditional in person theatre the idea is that you sell tickets, and a show makes money. It is possible to sell tickets for virtual shows, but most virtual theatre shows will end up as being watchable for free on social media platforms.

If we put our business hats on for a minute, I would suggest you view your virtual theatre projects as being in the same space as podcasts, YouTubers, TikTokers or other content creators. People who do content creation can make money from their projects, and they do so in a variety of ways.

Let's go over some ideas of how you could make money from your virtual theatre shows

Funding

You could try exploring if there are funding pots available that will support virtual theatre performances. This could either be from national or local arts councils, or other charitable organisations. Funding can be extremely competitive to get, so make sure you do your research and that you produce a pitch that will meet the goals and requirements of the organisation you are applying to.

Tickets

Social media platforms and even video meeting software companies such as Zoom are adding ways to make online events ticketed. Explore what is on offer from the various platforms, or you could use a dedicated ticket site like Eventbrite or Ticket Source.

If you sell tickets to shows, it would be unlikely that you would also broadcast it live to social media. Instead, it would only be viewable to audience members who would either join the video meeting as a non-video participant, or watch an unlisted social media video that you send to them.

Before rushing to sell tickets to virtual shows, I would suggest you do a few free shows, and/or lots of rehearsals to make sure you know how to put on a great show.

Keep in mind that if people are going to pay for tickets to a virtual theatre show in advance, you'll need to make sure that the show you put on gives value for money. If there are technical issues, or you create a show that isn't suited for virtual performance, it may be the last time people are willing to pay to see it.

Crowdfunding

If you have a big project you are working towards, you could consider some kind of crowdfunding campaign on sites like Kickstarter or Indiegogo. On these sites, you create a pitch for people to see what project you are planning, and you set funding goals.

For example, you could say that if you raise £1,000 you'll put on a series of five performances, and that the money would be used to pay cast, crew and for advertising and equipment. Then you could say that if you manage to raise £10,000, you'll create twenty performances, with extra cast and include special effects using a new technological gadget.

To incentivise people to become backers, you can offer various perks depending on the size of their donation. For example, you could say if you give £5, we'll thank you on our website, but if you give £10 we'll personally thank you at the end of a show. If they give £20 they will get a T-shirt with a logo of the show on it, and if they pledge £100 you'll let them play a small role in your show.

These are examples, but you see the kinds of things that you can offer.

Donations – Regular or one off

A popular way for content creators to make money is by receiving one off or regular donations from supporters of their work. Sites like Patreon, or Ko-fi allow people to make donations to content creators, and you can give backers access to exclusive content in return for their support.

T-shirts and other merch

You should consider setting up an online shop for your theatre company or show so that people can buy merchandise. If you have T-shirts or other merch like bags, cushion covers or phone cases with a show or company logo on, this can be a great way to earn with a show.

You may need to get someone to design logos or artwork for you, or you may have someone in your company who would be willing to do this for you. Having this in place will not only earn you money, but also give fans something physical that they can have to show they support your work. As an added bonus, if they wear a logo shirt, they will be a walking advert for your company!

20: THE TYPES OF SHOWS THAT WORK/DON'T WORK

What kinds of shows work for virtual theatre? And which ones don't? These are important questions, and the truth is, with enough practice, development and determination, any kind of show can translate well to virtual theatre. But this said, some certainly do lend themselves to work better/worse than others virtually.

Scripted plays

These can work perfectly well as virtual theatre. Actors may learn lines, or these could be performed as play readings. A competent technician could control which performers are in focus on a virtual stage, and add audio and visual effects to create a sense of atmosphere or location.

The plays that will work best virtually are ones that are written specifically with virtual theatre in mind. Radio plays should also work very well, although the added element of being able to see performers may be an advantage or disadvantage depending how much the radio play is benefited by being in the mind's eye of the audience. Theatre plays can also work fine, but you may need to make adjustments to ensure scenes with heavy stage directions can be translated to the restrictions of virtual theatre.

Musicals

Musicals will present all the same challenges as scripted plays, plus plenty more of their own. The biggest challenge of staging any musical virtually will be how you approach balancing the audio levels of singers and the music they are singing to. Performers will have to set up their own mics, and whether you have live music played by musicians, or played via a backing track, your technician will have their work cut out for them to make sure everything can be heard and is balanced correctly.

Additionally, musicals usually feature dancing, and whilst showing performers dancing via their webcams is possible, this would require sufficient space to do so. Also, partner dancing wouldn't be possible.

The biggest challenge with staging a virtual musical would be if there is lag on the internet connection. If people singing together don't hear the music or each other at the same time, it could lead to a mess. I do expect as internet speeds and computer technology improves that this will become less and less of an issue.

Improvised theatre

Of all the types of show on this list, I believe improv works the best virtually. I am biased of course, as you'll have noticed that this book is titled the Extreme Improv Ultimate Guide to Creating Virtual Theatre.

Improv initially seems as if it may not work virtually, as it usually relies on audience suggestions and interaction. But the reasons improv works so well virtually are many.

Using the chat function of social media platforms, you can still get audience suggestions to inspire scenes. Improv also lends itself to things being a little unpredictable or rough around the edges as by its nature it is not rehearsed. This means improv can easily acknowledge and make a strength out of any technical issues as part of the fun.

Improv can come in many forms such as short form sketch-based improv and long form plays and musicals. Improv also usually features a lot of mime work. Sets and props are usually played in the audience's mind's eye, so the lack of physical props, sets or locations doesn't affect improv online.

Stand-up comedy

Stand-up can work well virtually, but its real success may come down to the performance style of the individual comic. Some comics may find their timing is off or jokes feel flat when performed virtually. Even though stand-up is essentially a monologue and seems like it would translate well to a virtual space, in reality a stand-up comic is directly having a dialogue with the audience.

The lack of laughter or audience reaction can change the feel of stand-up done virtually but is achievable if a comic's material and performance style is adapted to work with no instant reaction.

Poetry

Poetry works incredibly well virtually. Poetry is most frequently done as a type of monologue, although multiple people sometimes perform poems together. Without the pressure or expectation that it needs to be funny, it doesn't miss that atmosphere of an audience in the same way that stand-up does.

Monologues

Like poetry, monologues also work very well online. Monologues are performed by individuals and therefore won't be hindered by the technology required to connect people over a video call. Performing a monologue virtually is essentially the same as doing a self-tape, which actors frequently have to do.

Storytelling

Storytelling can either be done as an individual, or as a collective. Depending on this, it will change how challenging storytelling is to stage virtually. If there is just one person it will be like doing a monologue or poetry, and if there are more people, it will be closer to performing a play.

Storytellers often will speak directly to an audience, and this is easily achieved by talking directly into a webcam.

Puppet shows

Performing with puppets online has challenges but works surprisingly well. Perhaps the biggest challenge of it is that a puppeteer would need to be able to see their computer screen to make sure the puppet is framed properly, whilst also making sure they are not visible in the shot.

Ventriloquism may be something that works very well, as both the puppet and puppeteer would be able to be seen at the same time. This would create a rare example of where virtual theatre would have two people in the same frame at the same time...even if one is a puppet.

Children's theatre

Children's theatre performed virtually will be a mix of a play, improv and may have puppetry or musical elements. These can work very well virtually, although may require more in the way of props, costume or visual effects and music to keep a child's attention.

Dance shows

As discussed when talking about musicals, dance based shows are possible, but the performers would need adequate space to dance in, and unless you have multiple people in the same physical location, you wouldn't be able to do any dance routines that require physical interaction or cooperation.

Singing based shows

Singing shows would have all the technical challenges of putting on a virtual musical. Balancing audio levels and making sure mics and other tech is all working together properly is essential.

The benefit of a singing based shows is that it is likely to have an Emcee and breaks between songs to introduce the next act. This element reduces the pressure you'd find with a musical where scenes and songs would need to flow seamlessly from one to another. This can allow vital time to address any tech concerns between songs.

Magic or other variety acts

Magic shows online can work very well, but may depend on the type of magic tricks being performed. If certain tricks require space, or audience interaction these may need adjusting to work virtually.

Other variety acts such as ones where people do physical feats, or work with animals could work very well, but again, may depend on available space.

Gameshows, Chat shows and Panel shows

Gameshows and chat and panel shows can work really well virtually. Presentation wise, these will often seem like video podcasts, and the main challenges are for the Emcee to oversee that the conversation continues to flow and if there are multiple guests, that it is clear who is speaking to who.

Gameshows in particular may benefit from extra design elements like scoreboards, or onscreen information such as questions or timers. These are very achievable in virtual shows.

21: TIPS FOR RUNNING TECH ON A VIRTUAL THEATRE SHOW

If you are running tech on a virtual theatre show, you will effectively be taking on many roles all at once. This may include the roles of director, camera operator, director of photography, and sound and lighting operator.

Running a live virtual theatre show is like running a live television broadcast. You will find that you are in charge of what camera view is being shown, when on screen text and titles are displayed and if any sound or graphics need playing.

In this section we'll go over the specific controls for several of the programmes we've covered. Here are some general tips for some of the universal tasks you'll need to do regardless of which application you are using.

Spotlighting performers

One of the main things the person running the tech will need to do during a virtual show is ensure that the audience know who to focus on at any given moment. This will usually mean spotlighting or pinning performers, so they are shown more prominently on screen.

This is a simple enough action in most applications, but the real skill comes in getting the timing of spotlighting people, and doing it efficiently. If a character is due to enter or exit a scene, you'll want to make sure you add or remove them quickly so that there isn't an awkward or unnatural pause whilst tech things happen.

To use breakout rooms or not?

You could have breakout rooms set up to use as a virtual backstage area. Breakout rooms look and feel like a regular meeting, but unless the host/person streaming the show enters one, they wouldn't be visible to the audience.

I wouldn't suggest using breakout rooms in most instances. It would mean you wouldn't know what is happening in the show if you were in a breakout room. If you have your camera off, you are effectively in the wings, waiting to go on stage. A breakout room is like a dressing room which has no monitor.

If you are part of a variety show, or stand-up show where different acts come on that are separate from each other, it may be useful to have a breakout room until shortly before you're going on stage. Even then, I'd be more inclined to be ready in the wings and know what's going on than not.

Onscreen graphics

A technician will also oversee making sure any onscreen graphics display at the right time. This may be as simple as highlighting comments from viewers, which is available to do in some software, or loading graphics or text to display from dedicated broadcasting software.

Once again, getting the timing of these and making them display in a smooth fashion is essential for a well-produced show. The best advice I can give is for the technician to know as much as possible what may be needed during a show and being organised to know how to quickly access the graphics.

This may include having lists of graphics and effects clearly organised in the broadcasting software or taking the time to learn or create hotkey short cuts. A Stream Deck device, or equivalent, as mentioned in chapter 8 is fantastic way to control most aspects of a show, and in particular can make accessing graphics and other media a breeze.

Soundchecks

One of the responsibilities of the technician will be to make sure the show is broadcasting as intended on the social media platforms.

A technician who is streaming the show from their computer should check everyone's audio levels when they join the video meeting. If anyone is very quiet, too loud, or having any crackles or interference, you'll want to trouble shoot this as best you can before you go live.

Unfortunately, to some degree, it will be down to the individual performer to fix any audio issues they are having, as they alone will be able to change their mic or play with their own computer's audio settings. But the technician can still advise, and most importantly, be the person responsible for identifying any issues or imbalances.

A technician should also ensure that even if the performers can hear each other through the video meeting, that the audience can hear the show when it goes live. This is something you won't be able to know for certain until you actually go live, and the best way to check it is to use a phone or tablet to listen and check that people can be heard.

If you have a pre-show scene setup, you could display a soundcheck notice for any viewers, and run a quick soundcheck before a show actually begins. This is something that normally would happen before an audience enter an in-person theatre, but unfortunately is something that can only be fully tested when you go live on a virtual theatre show.

This may feel a tad unprofessional to allow the audience to hear performers doing a soundcheck before a show officially begins. If you display a disclaimer that this is what is happening, and plan what the performers will say in the soundcheck you can make it a stylised extension of the show. I would view this process as similar to a band tuning up before a musical, which often can be heard by the audience as they enter a theatre, and can add to the anticipation of what is going on.

Other technical checks

Before you go live, check that everyone can see and hear each other, and do what you can to troubleshoot any issues anyone is having. If someone is having audio or video problems, make sure they have the latest updates to any software you are using, or advise them to close any programs down that aren't required for the show. If they still have issues, see if they can join the meeting from an alternative device.

Once the show has gone live, you'll want to make sure the video and sound are coming through as expected on the social media platforms, and also that the titles and descriptions of any live shows are named correctly so that audience members can easily search and find the show.

What to do if there are technical difficulties

Technical difficulties happen all the time, and sometimes there is nothing you can do about them. If they happen, don't panic. There are usually many solutions to any and every problem.

Have a plan before the show starts

Say for example, if you are mid show and one performer loses their internet connection, or freezes on screen, you'll need to evaluate if the show can continue without them. Ideally you should discuss any such eventuality before a show, and come up with a plan for how you will handle this.

Acknowledge technical issues if you can continue with something else

For some types of show, such as improv or podcasts or variety acts you should just be able to go to the next performer, and even acknowledge that the person is having slight issues before you continue.

Improvise if you have to

If you are doing something scripted, the performers may be able to continue by improvising to allow time for someone to solve their tech issue. Remember that unless the audience know your script, they may not realise that there was ever an issue if you carry on like any mistakes were meant to happen.

See if a performer can join from another device

If a performer is having issues, they may benefit from joining the meeting from a different computer, phone or tablet, or using a different internet connection. If this isn't possible, or doesn't work, they should try resetting their computer and/or their internet connection. This can take time, so it may be time to put the show on pause and go to an unscheduled interval.

Be honest and display technical difficulties if there is no other option

If, however, the show cannot continue without a particular performer, I would suggest you have a scene or overlay setup and ready to display that says 'Technical difficulties' and that the show will resume shortly.

This idea will also hold true if for example you find that there are sound issues, or that the video is glitching or playing with a poor frame rate. Don't panic and take as long as it needs to fix issues and continue when you've resolved them

What to do if you the technical difficulties are on your end, and you're the one streaming the show?

If things are running slow or glitchy, I would suggest you go onto your technical difficulties screen whilst you try to resolve them. If you don't think you can, you may need to restart your computer or internet connection. Doing this will end the stream.

If you have no better option than to end the stream, attempt to have one of the cast, Emcee or technician address the audience and let them know the situation if possible. This can either be on camera, just with audio, or just with an onscreen text display.

It's not ideal, but people will understand if there are technical difficulties. Just let them know that you are planning a break for a few minutes to resolve the issue and that they should stick around and check your social media channels for updates on when the show will resume.

If a show just crashes and you are unable to warn the audience

If a stream shuts down, you should see if you can get it back online as soon as possible. Take a moment to evaluate if you need to restart your computer or internet, and that it won't just crash again if you think there will be ongoing issues.

Whilst you are doing this, I would suggest you go to your social media channels and make a quick announcement that you have suffered a technical error, and that you are working hard to get the show back online as soon as possible.

What if a show crashes on your end and you cannot get it back online?

If you are streaming the show and you have major computer issues and it is not possible for you to continue streaming the show yourself, you still have a few options before it's all over.

If you were streaming from a home internet connection, consider if you have mobile phone internet and whether it is feasible to continue streaming using that as a hotspot. Depending on speed, and internet allowance this may not be possible.

Say you were using Zoom as the video meeting for your show, do you have an alternative device such as a phone or tablet that you could try streaming the meeting directly from? If your computer is having the issue, this would allow you to continue the show, although you may lose the benefit of any graphics, music or overlays that you designed in the broadcasting software.

One solution here may be to abandon streaming live and simply record the meeting. You may then be able to edit together the show with any overlays and effects later. This may create significant extra work.

Question if someone else could take over the streaming side of things from their computer or device. This may mean that the other person doesn't have the same broadcasting software or knowledge as you, but if your priority is to get the show back online as quickly as possible this may be the fastest solution.

Finally, you may have to accept that whilst you may lose a battle, you will live to fight another day

If you've explored all of these options and are not getting anywhere, it may be best to call it a day, and accept that your stream is not going live today. You can then take time to regroup and reschedule the show for another day.

One of the great things about virtual theatre shows is that they are easier to reschedule than live in person shows or film shoots. As the performers can in theory join a show from all over the world, and audiences can watch from anywhere, or watch on demand, you don't have the pressure of getting everyone together to a specific location all at the same time.

Take a day and you may find your computer or internet issues can be resolved, or that you need to change a setting or two to get things up and running. Whatever the issue was, the good news is that there is always a solution and you should be able to get things back up on their feet in no time.

Zoom Specific tips

If you are using Zoom for your video meeting, there are several things you can control live during the show. Let's break them down.

Don't be the only host

The most important tip I can give for Zoom users if you are running the tech is to make sure others in the Zoom meeting are set as co-hosts. If there are any technical difficulties on your end and things freeze up, or the software crashes, Zoom will automatically end the meeting and kick everyone out unless someone else is set as a co-host. Doing this will allow you to quickly re-join the meeting and pick up where you left off without having to setup a new meeting and get everyone back to join again.

Layout – Speaker vs gallery view

If you move the mouse to the top right of the screen in Zoom, you should see an icon for the 'View' menu. Clicking this will bring up options for speaker, gallery and immersive views.

I wouldn't suggest using speaker view for virtual theatre shows. Speaker view will automatically spotlight whoever is speaking, but this can easily be interrupted if someone coughs or makes a noise. That person would then be spotlighted and take the focus off someone who you may want the focus to be on.

For the most part, I would suggest that you leave the show in gallery mode. This will show everyone in the meeting in equal size boxes on the screen at the same time, unless you purposely choose to spotlight people.

Show non video participants

Additionally, I would also suggest that you disable the option to show non video participants. To do this click the ^ symbol next to the camera control at the bottom of the screen and choose video settings. Now from the pop-up menu check the hide non video participants option.

Doing this will mean that if a participant stops their video, it will hide the window where their webcam was shown. If you choose to show non video participants, an empty window will remain in the absence of the person who turned their webcam off.

The only reason you may want to leave 'show non video participants' on is if having a set layout of where everyone is on screen and the size of the windows needs to remain consistent.

Change the positioning and order of people on the screen

You can click and drag people around on screen to change and swap their position. If you do this, it may not initially display the same for everyone. To make sure it does, click the view menu icon at the top right of the screen and click on 'follow host's video order'. You'll also notice that you can 'release host's video order' as well.

Spotlighting participants

From being in gallery view, hover your mouse over the webcam of any of the participants and you will see a three-dot menu icon in the corner. Click this and you will be able to choose to spotlight that participant. Do this with one participant and it will make the view of them largest on the screen, and it will place everyone else into a "backline area" at the top of the screen.

Click on additional participants at the top and you'll be able to add a spotlight to them as well. You can remove spotlights by clicking on their three-dot menu and choosing remove spotlight. To remove all spotlights go to the view menu in the top right of the screen and choose 'remove all spotlights'.

Layout – Immersive view

Click the view icon and choose immersive view. This will bring up a pop-up window where you can select from a range of scene settings that Zoom offers, or you can upload your own. To choose your own, click the + symbol and select an image from your hard drive.

When in immersive view, the participant's backgrounds will be removed to give a greater sense that they are in the same virtual environment.

If you find that someone's room is still showing, check that they have the latest update to Zoom installed. Also ask them to go into their video settings and check that in the 'backgrounds and effects' tab, make sure the 'I have a greenscreen' box is unchecked.

Immersive view can give the sense that the performers are in the same space together. If you are running tech, you will have the ability to click on the view of any of the performers and drag them around the screen. If done well, you can create the illusion that characters are moving about the screen. As a host or co-host of the meeting you can only move one participant at a time.

You can also resize a participant's webcam to create the sense of some characters being bigger or smaller, or being near or far from the camera. Clicking the X in the corner of a person's webcam will take that person out of the immersive view and place them in the backline area along the top of the screen.

Screensharing audio

If you want to play music or other sound cues that everyone in the meeting will be able to hear, you can do this by screensharing your audio. Click the share screen button and then click advanced. Here you will see the option to share computer audio. Click it and then click share.

I would then suggest you play any audio cues you want both the audience and the other participants to hear through a media player. Have these ready to go in a playlist or selectable from an easy to access folder and they should play after perhaps a short time delay.

Chat window

As I discussed in the designing your show in Zoom chapter, I would recommend always having the chat and participants menu open so you can privately communicate with others in the show during the stream.

Having the ability to send private messages to the cast can be very valuable in terms of communicating any technical concerns, or getting timing in shows correct.

If you are running tech, and presumably also streaming the show from your computer, there is a chance that opening and closing the chat window may change the way Zoom is displayed in your broadcasting software. By having the window always open, you will have been able to design your show around this.

If you are streaming the show directly from Zoom, having the chat and participants window open will not change how the meeting is displayed on the stream.

Muting participants

If you hover the mouse cursor over any participant, you'll see the option to mute them. This may be useful if there is sound interference coming from the environment that person is in, and that person is not in the current scene. They will be able to unmute themselves, but if you have muted them, it may be worth using the chat to private message and say that they have been muted as they may not realise.

If you mute a participant, or they mute themselves, only the muted person will be able to unmute themselves. You cannot unmute someone without their knowledge for privacy reasons.

Stopping a participant's cameras

Just as you can mute someone, the host can click on the three-dot menu on each person's webcam view, and you'll see the option to stop their video. Once again, you will not be able to start their video feed for them, and as the host you'll only be able to request someone start their webcam again.

Skype Specific Tips

Skype is limited in the controls it offers a technician to work with. Here are some things you can do.

Change the position of participants/layout of the screen

You can move the position of participants on screen by dragging and dropping them, however this only worked for me on the phone/tablet editions of the software at the time of writing.

To change the layout, go to the view icon at the top right of the screen and select between speaker, grid and together mode views.

Cropped view mode

You can make it so that the participants webcams fill the screen without any black bars by clicking the three-dot menu next to their name and choosing 'see full video feed'.

Together Mode

Together mode will add participants to a virtual set, but you cannot add your own image at time of writing.

Virtual Backgrounds

These are added by individual users from the video settings menu. Click the three-dots next to your name and choose change background to do this.

Screensharing

Click the share screen button from the tools under the meeting view and you'll be able to choose a monitor display or open window/programme to share the view of.

Google Meet specific tips

Google Meet offers very limited tools currently.

Spotlighting participants

From the three-dot menu, choose layout and you can choose between a tiled view to see everyone on screen at once, or spotlight/sidebar to put the focus on an individual.

To spotlight a specific individual, hover your mouse over their webcam and choose the pin icon to put them in focus.

Currently you can only spotlight one person at a time. This means that two hander scenes are problematic if you have a larger cast. The best option is to use the tiles view to show two or more participants at the same time, but you cannot currently select to exclude someone from the tiled layout. Even if they switch their webcam off, their profile picture will still display.

The only exception to this rule is if you are the person streaming the view of the Google Meet video call. You can hover over your webcam and choose to minimise it to remove your own webcam from the grid of tiles. You cannot do this to other people's even if you're the host, and if others minimise their own camera, it only minimises it for themselves.

Filters and virtual backgrounds

Users on smart devices can add Snapchat style filters to change the colour and tone of their webcam and add virtual hats and other costumes to themselves. This was not available on the computer browser version of the software at the time of writing.

Both smart device and computer users can add virtual backgrounds from the 'apply visual effects' option from the three-dot menu.

OBS/Stream Labs Specific Tips

Organise any onscreen graphics and music cues

Under the list of sources will be a list of all the elements you've put into the creation of your show. The order they are listed in will dictate their order as layers. If you have any video trailers, lower thirds or images you wish to display as pop-ups on your show, make sure these are listed as the top layers, so they display correctly and are easy to find.

Also, any music/audio cues you wish to access to play should be listed together so you can quickly find these as well.

Both pop-up elements and audio cues could be placed together or in separate group folders for ease of access.

This will make scrolling through the sources and finding anything you may need to display or play throughout the show easy. To toggle on/off any elements, just click the eye icon next to the name of the element to make it visible or not.

Hotkeys

An easier way to switch on/off elements that you may need to access is through assigning hotkeys to them. In both OBS/SLOBS this can be done in the settings menu. Access the settings menu in OBS by clicking the settings under the controls tab, or in SLOBS by clicking the settings cog icon.

When the menu pops up, you'll see the hotkeys tab, and be able to assign any key to toggle the source on/off.

Keep an eye on the audio levels to make sure they're working

Before going live with a show, you should check that audio is coming through into the software correctly. The audio mixer will show a list of any audio sources that you have as part of the show. This will include desktop audio, any mics you have added as a source and also any audio and video media you might play in the show.

If you are performing or will otherwise need to be heard in the show, you should check that your mic is coming through. Under the audio mixer you will see the volume metre for your mic source bounce up and down as you speak into it.

Also check to see if the desktop audio volume metre shows sound coming through when people on the show speak.

You may wish to slide your volume lower or higher to match the volume of the video meeting source, so they come through at a balanced volume. Remember, when using OBS/SLOBS in conjunction with a video meeting software such as Zoom, that even if you can hear the other people in the Zoom meeting, the audience won't be able to hear you unless you add a mic source into the broadcasting software.

Lastly, you should make sure that any audio cues such as music or sound effects are switched off before you begin. It will be easy to notice if a video or graphic is playing when it shouldn't be as it will be visible in the stream preview window. With audio, it can be easy to have something playing so it can be heard to the audience, but not to the person streaming.

If you wear headphones whilst running a show, you could have it so audio cues play out loud and you hear them through the headphones, but if you're not using headphones and audio cues play out loud through your speakers, you will end up with an echo of music as it is picked up by your mic.

When I do shows I am performing in, I usually don't wear headphones as I find them restricting. I will just output the audio to the stream and not monitor it through my computer speakers. Whatever approach you take, make sure you check audio levels in the mixer and that nothing is accidentally playing that you don't want to be.

StreamYard Specific Tips

StreamYard offer a limited number of tools for a technician to learn to use during a live show.

Host/Admin Controls

When cast members join the call in StreamYard, they will appear in a backstage area, and not be seen by the audience unless added to take part in the live show. Adding cast members onto the live show is as simple as hovering over them and clicking 'add to stream' or 'remove from stream' to do the reverse and put them into the backstage area.

Users can only add people to the stream from the backstage area if they are the owner of the stream, or if they have been set as an admin or co-host. To do this, you have to go to the members area when you log in to the website. From there you can invite people to accept these roles.

Non owner/admin/co-host guests in the meeting can still choose to switch off their own camera view, and they can remove themselves from the screen into the backstage area, but they cannot add themselves back onto the virtual stage.

Spotlighting cast

To spotlight a cast member, click on the three dots icon to bring up controls for that person and choose 'solo layout'. To exit the solo layout view, just repeat the process and choose exit solo layout.

Change the layout of the stream

People with admin/co-host roles can also change the layout of the stream. Just under the view of the Ustream are the layout options. The solo person icon will just show the first participant listed in the meeting. This is usually the host, but if the host's camera is off it will default to the next person whose webcam is on.

Cropped layout will show all participants side by side with no view of any backgrounds. The view you get of each webcam will focus on the centre and crop the sides off.

Changing people's on-screen positions

If you want to change the order of people on the screen, you can simply drag and move them with your mouse to change/swap their positions.

Muting cast

Cast can mute themselves, or you can mute them by hitting the mic icon on each cast member. Do note, that the technician/host cannot unmute a participant in the meeting and if muted, they will have to unmute themselves.

Video clips and Screensharing

Assuming you already have any video clips loaded into the show (as discussed in the designing your show on StreamYard section of the book) just click the videos you wish to play from the video clips section of the brand part of the side panel.

If you are screensharing clips or images, have these clips ready to go and click share. Choose the monitor you have the clips ready on and they will display. As mentioned in an earlier section, screensharing is best if you have multiple monitors so you can give the smoothest experience. If you have just one monitor, you will end up showing the meeting controls in screen share mode.

Restream Studio specific tips

There are limited tools to play around with in Restream Studio, but there are still some useful features that are unique to the service.

Layout

Under the stream preview window there are various layout designs to pick from. These include side by side views, and cropped view which will crop the webcam views so they fill the screen and sit next to each other. There are also useful picture in picture and thumbnail views to allow greater focus on one performer.

Swapping cast member positions

If you would like to swap the positions of the cast, all you need to do is drag and drop them into position.

Stop camera/Muting other participants

A feature which I have found to be unique to Restream Studio is that the host of the meeting has greater ability to stop/restart a participant's devices if they choose.

If you are the host and you stop another person's microphone or exit them into the backstage area, you will be able to toggle them back on to be seen/heard in the show again. Technically, if a participant stops their camera or mic themselves, the host will not be able to start them up again. Regardless, this does still give the host greater control than on other software we have explored. This could lead to a participant seeing that they are in the backstage area or that they are muted and they may suddenly find they can be seen or heard again when they are not ready.

Screensharing

Clicking the screenshare icon from the options under the stream preview will allow you to select any monitor display or open application on your computer.

Highlighting chat messages, captions and video clips

In the chat tab in the righthand panel, the host can choose to toggle on/off the chat overlay, or just click on individual messages to highlight them onscreen.

The host also has the ability to display on screen messages, such as please subscribe, or play video clips such as intro sequences or establishing shots between scenes. You could also use full screen overlays to display adverts or 'be right back' screens.

Private chat

Host/cast/crew can communicate with each other via the private chat feature in Restream Studio.

Twitch Studio specific tips

If you are handling the tech for your show and are using Twitch Studio, here are some useful tips.

Changing and editing scenes during a show

The scene list for the stream is in the left panel next to the stream preview. Changing scenes is as simple as a clicking on their title. You can also assign hot keys for changing scenes in the settings menu.

If there are onscreen elements you need to activate/deactivate, just click 'Edit' next to the name of the scene you are currently on. Note that you cannot edit a different scene during the live broadcast as opening the editor for a different scene will change it so that you are displaying that scene instead.

Examples of elements you may need to switch on/off during a live show may include title cards to show the name of a location or scene, or if your show requires an onscreen timer.

To toggle any element on/off, hover over the name of that element in the layers tab and you will see an eye icon. Click it to switch it between visible/invisible.

Timer

The Timer can be toggled visible/invisible in the same method as the other onscreen elements, but it has unique extra controls in the editor. In the right-hand panel, you can change the duration, and start/pause or reset the timer.

Screensharing

Though called 'Screensharing' in Twitch Studio, what you actually do is choose to import a desktop view, or view of any open application. It combines the ability of display capture and window capture as seen in other software and puts them both under the title of screensharing.

You shouldn't confuse this with screensharing that is done in the likes of Zoom, or Microsoft Teams, as only the person running the stream will see it live. Audience members will see what you are screensharing on a slight time delay, and the cast members in your video call meeting won't see it at all. You will have to use the screenshare feature in the video meeting software for the participants to see your screen.

Draw mode

A neat feature in Twitch Studio is draw mode. Draw mode can be activated with the little squiggly icon at the top right of the stream preview window. This will bring up colour and brush tools and will allow the person running the stream to draw across the stream with their mouse pointer.

This could be useful for a fun Pictionary like game with your viewers during the pre-show or interval. You could draw something and the audience could guess what you're drawing in the comments section.

It could also be useful during certain types of show, if you want to do some basic art (the tools are very limited) or if you want to highlight things onscreen with circles or arrows. There is a handy trashcan icon to clear all the drawings off the screen.

Note that what you draw on the screen will not be visible to cast members if they are in a Zoom or other video call meeting.

22: RUNNING A VIRTUAL THEATRE SHOW – AS AN EMCEE

Not every type of virtual theatre show will need or benefit from having an Emcee or host, but there are plenty of types of show where one would be useful. These include improv, stand-up, gameshows, podcasts, variety shows, and even some plays or musicals may benefit from an introduction, or to provide post show information, chats and Q&As.

Here are some tips and tricks to do well if you are the Emcee of a virtual theatre show.

Get your eyeline right

If you are addressing the audience at home, look directly into the lens of your webcam. This may mean you are not looking at other performers in your video call, but it will help establish to the audience when you are speaking directly to them.

If you are speaking to other people in the video meeting, feel free to look at them on the computer screen. Your eyeline will move (usually down as webcams are most frequently placed above a monitor) and this subtle difference in where you are looking will help the audience understand who you are talking to.

You could turn your head to one side to more clearly communicate a direction of who you are talking to, but doing this may mean you cannot actually see your monitor. This may be useful to simulate two characters being in the same room together, but isn't necessary for most situations where an Emcee would be needed.

Your personality and energy will fill the gap of a missing audience

Unlike in real life theatres or television studios, a virtual show is very unlikely to have crowd noise and the sense of atmosphere that a live audience can create. For comedy or light-hearted shows, this can create a sense of emptiness. Jokes without laughter may feel that they land flat. If you are used to presenting to a live crowd, you may find that there is a difference in energy and your rhythm when you are just in front of a webcam.

As the Emcee of a virtual show, you'll want to keep the energy of the show feeling positive, and you can do this by staying engaged with the others on the show. Show an interest in any messages that come in from the comments/chat section. If you seem interested in what is going on, you will project this sense of engagement to the audience as well. After all, why would the audience want to stick around if the host doesn't seem that interested themselves?

Know what you need to communicate to the audience

If you are the Emcee of your own show, or if you have been asked to Emcee for someone else, make sure you know what you are aiming to achieve with the show. If you are doing introductions, make sure you know the relevant information of what you are introducing. If you need to let the audience know a web address, or times and dates of your next show, have that information ready.

Basically, do all you can to remove any barriers that would prevent the audience getting the information you want them to have and that may stop them enjoying the show. Be concise, but don't be afraid to repeat information multiple times to make sure things are clear.

A difference between in person theatre and virtual theatre is that at live theatre shows, the audience will all have paid for tickets and be seated before the show begins. This means they are more likely to be invested in paying attention to the show, as they have paid to do so. They will have seen the show from the start, but this isn't necessarily the case with virtual theatre.

Most virtual theatre shows that are performed are watchable for free on YouTube etc. People may also tune in 5 minutes late, or even an hour late. They are also more likely to be distracted by things or people around them. Both the Emcee and cast overall will need to do what they can to keep the audience engaged, and make sure they understand what they are watching.

Once again, be concise with your message, but don't be afraid to repeat information multiple times. Reiterating the name of your show or company will ensure new viewers know what they are watching. Also remind people that they should click the like, follow or subscribe buttons to help you achieve your goals to keep and grow your audience.

Keep an eye on the chat

Unless you have comments disabled on your video, the audience will be able to post comments in the comments/live chat section of the site you are streaming to. As the Emcee of a show, you'll be able to get a sense of how engaged an audience is form the comments section.

If there are no comments, it may be that you are running the kind of show where people are simply just watching and not thinking about putting comments during a show. For some producers, directors and performers that will be their preference. But do keep in mind that virtual theatre is a medium that lends itself to audience engagement and interaction.

If there are comments coming through, the Emcee, or another company member could take the opportunity to type messages back and encourage those commenting to further engage with the show. The Emcee may also choose to answer audience comments verbally on the show. Giving shout outs to individuals, or answering questions is an important way to build an audience and get a connection with them in a virtual show.

Juggling running tech and being the Emcee at the same time

It's very common that the person who is the Emcee of a virtual theatre show may also be the person running the tech and streaming the show from their computer. This makes sense as virtual theatre makes it easy for producers to create new shows quickly, and if you want to make a show, you are more likely to take on these roles to see it happen.

Balancing these roles can take time to learn, and you may decide to delegate one or more of them to someone else. Doing this is fine. A problem shared is a problem halved as the saying goes.

But let's assume you want to be the Emcee of your show, and also have the control and responsibility of setting up the stream and running the tech too.

It's very possible, but you do have to be aware that splitting your focus between tasks may impact one or all of them. This isn't to say you shouldn't do multiple tasks, as when it comes to Extreme Improv virtual shows, I will Emcee, perform, run tech and run the stream all at once.

So, using myself as an example, how do I juggle all these tasks?

To begin with, I recognise that Extreme Improv XStreamed shows are comedy based where I have the ability to reference any "mistakes" and turn the mistakes into jokes. The cast and audience all are made aware that I'm fulfilling all these roles, and in my unique style, I run with anything that happens be it good, bad or downright ugly. In true improv style I say 'yes and' to pretty much everything.

This won't work for everyone, but I will add a certain amount of narration to any technical tasks I am handling throughout a show. It fills gaps, and builds anticipation of what is about to happen. This wouldn't work in a play, but for my comedy shows it works just fine.

I would say both being the Emcee and running the tech side of things gives me an advantage over others who just Emcee. I will be aware of anything technical that is happening. This means I'll have much greater accuracy and timing for technical things such spotlighting myself or others in scenes.

23: TIPS FOR PERFORMING IN A VIRTUAL THEATRE SHOW

If you are a performer who will be appearing in a virtual theatre show, you will find that there are adjustments you need to make compared to how you perform on a real-world stage. These changes may take some time to learn or get used to, but it is just another skill you can add to your acting toolbox, just as it is to learn to perform for radio or film.

Tech things a performer will need to do

In the past, an actor could always leave the tech side of things to the technician. The camera operator and DOP would set up the shots, and if a mic goes wrong, or if a light goes out, it would be up to the technical crew to solve. The actor meanwhile can go wait in their dressing room.

But during a virtual theatre show, a performer will have to set up their own camera and lights. The technician operating the show will only be able to do so much and this will mainly be from an advisory perspective.

Basic conditions for your setup

I've covered what tech you'll need elsewhere in the book, but just to reiterate, you'll need your device – either a computer or smart device. You'll then need to set it up somewhere with good lighting, as much space as you need to perform, and somewhere that you'll have good internet signal and isn't too noisy.

Positioning your camera

When you perform in virtual theatre shows, you will also take on some of the responsibilities of a camera operator, director, and lighting technician. Others may advise you, but you'll have to set it all up.

Ideally, you'll want your webcam set up to be about eye level for where you'll be sat or stood. Some prefer to stand, and others sit whilst performing. This is something we'll discuss in more depth in a little while. If you have your webcam lower than your eyeline, you may start to get unflattering camera angles. Unless you want the audience to see up your nose or get the impression that you have a wider neck than in reality, make sure you have an eye level camera.

If your camera is slightly higher than you, it may give the sense of the audience looking down on you and give a sense of lower status.

Framing wise, you should aim for your eye level to come about one third of the way down the screen. I've seen many performers where they have huge amounts of space above their heads, and this is all wasted space.

Using Zoom, Skype or another video meeting software

You'll need to familiarise yourself with Zoom, or whichever video conferencing software the company are using. They all work similar to each other but have differences. If you'll be using something you're not familiar with, it's better to ask for help and get someone to run through things with you before a show, than to find that you struggle mid show.

Here are the main things a performer may need to do tech wise during a show

Start/Stop your camera

If you're in a show where characters need to come and go from scenes, the best way to achieve this is by the actor stopping their own camera view. To do this, there will be a button onscreen called 'stop video' or something to this effect.

Stopping your camera view is like stepping off stage into the wings of a theatre. You will still be able to see and hear the other performers on stage and this will allow you to wait ready to go back on.

It is possible for a host or admin of the video meeting to stop another person's camera, but once done they wouldn't be able to restart that person's camera view again. This is so that video meeting users can keep their privacy and not have their cameras started when they are not ready.

This means the technician would only be able to request you start your camera again, and you'll still have to start it yourself. As such it's better if the responsibility of entering and exiting the virtual stage is always left to the performer.

A challenge this creates for the performer is that you'll need to get used to having your hand ready on the mouse or a hotkey to stop your camera at the end of the scene. If you can do this discreetly, it will avoid an awkward moment where the character is left hanging around. If not it may be noticeable that you are no longer in character and are trying to deal with tech.

It's understandable that having to work in a technical aspect like this does mean that you can't fully concentrate just on the acting. With practice it can become as natural looking and part of your routine as positioning yourself on stage or prepping yourself in stage combat.

Muting and unmuting yourself

This works very much the same as starting/stopping your camera. Your video call software will have a microphone button to start/stop the mic.

Unlike with the camera, the way you use it may be slightly different. If you are quiet, you should be fine to start your microphone a moment or two before you enter a scene. By doing this, you can make sure you will be able to be heard from the moment you switch on your camera, and you can even deliver some lines offstage to pre-empt your entrance.

When you exit a scene, I would suggest your stop your camera first, and then your mic as you can simply stay silent once your camera is off.

Here's a couple of warnings when it comes to operating your own mic.

It's a lot easier to forget to start your mic than it is to forget to start your camera. If you start your camera, you'll know because you'll be able to see that you are onscreen. Don't make the mistake of assuming that if you can be seen that you can also be heard. I think everyone who has ever done virtual theatre will have encountered the scenario where a performer has to be told 'You're on mute'.

And just like with the camera, the host won't be able to start your mic again for you due to privacy reasons.

The other warning is to make sure your mic is off when it doesn't need to be on. Some shows may benefit from leaving your mic on to provide laughter or atmosphere, but generally, if you're not in the scene, you don't need your mic on.

If you leave your mic on, and there is noticeable noise coming through, you can expect that the host/technician will mute you. Luckily, you can unmute yourself, but it can be easy to not notice you've been muted if you weren't the one to mute yourself.

If the host makes you a co-host or admin of the meeting

Sometimes the host of a meeting may make you a co-host/admin/team member of a video call.

Doing this can help in case of technical difficulties. If the host of a call loses their internet connection, everyone may find they are kicked out of the meeting, and the show is instantly dead in the water. By setting someone as co-host, the video meeting will keep going, and you can wait in the call until technical difficulties have been resolved.

Other reasons to give a performer co-host privileges is so they can share the controls to spotlight themselves or others, mute people and other tasks that the host/technician may normally do. I would give the warning to make sure everyone has the understanding of what is or is not acceptable for them to do in this manner.

If a performer starts spotlighting others, and the technician wasn't expecting it, or was trying to do it at the same time, this may lead to confusion or frustration between people.

Keep an eye on the text chat

Zoom, StreamYard and such like will allow participants of the video meeting to send group and private messages to each other in the video application.

This is useful to help coordinate cast and crew for anything you may need to relay to each other that you would normally be able to whisper backstage or talk through in a dressing room.

Working out timings for entrances can be given through chat, and will help keep everyone in sync. Text chat can also be used to warn others of technical issues, such as your mic being too quiet, or that you've forgotten a prop etc.

Some performers will find text chat messages popping up very distracting, but I would say it is better for them to be used than not. Depending on the show, it may be fine to use the text chat for fun or conversational messages, but maybe check this is acceptable before a show begins. Pointless chitter chatter could be seen as disrespectful to the performers on the virtual stage, distract them unnecessarily, or may mean they miss an important show related message.

Breakout rooms

As discussed in the tips for the technician, a virtual show could use breakout rooms as a kind of backstage area. If you consider that your camera being off is like waiting in the wings, a breakout room is like being in a dressing room with no live monitor of what is happening on stage.

Virtual backgrounds

I've detailed how to add virtual backgrounds in the designing your show sections of the book already (begins at chapter 13), so won't repeat those steps here. It should be noted that each performer will have to set their virtual backgrounds in whichever video conferencing software you are using. A host/technician cannot change this.

It's very easy to change your virtual background in most software and the controls to do this are usually in the video settings.

Depending how elaborate your show is, you may want to regularly change your virtual background to reflect changes in locations or mood. If you do a show where scenes move from place to place, you could have images ready of dining rooms, and bedrooms, or of Times Square or Big Ben to show that you are in these locations.

Make sure you check with the director of a show if it's appropriate to do this or not, because if you're the only one doing it in a large cast it may be distracting. Likewise, it may be that the director wants you to use specific images or videos at certain times. Make sure you have anything you'd need and know how to change between them before the show begins.

Having fun with greenscreens

If your video meeting software allows you to use greenscreens for virtual backgrounds, you may find there are ways in which you can have fun with the greenscreen technology. If you wear, or cover yourself with a green sheet or clothing, you will find that the greenscreen tech will make your covered body parts invisible. This can be fun for showing yourself as a floating head, or as someone without a head, or if you want to having objects floating about the screen in front of you.

VTubers, Snap Camera, and virtual filters/avatars

VTubers

If you're not familiar with the term VTuber, it means a virtual YouTuber, who will present on shows or just interact with their audience whilst using a virtual avatar.

There are several applications you can use on your computer to add filters to your webcam view, and this may include replacing yourself with a motion tracked virtual avatar. For several years this technology has been improving and many people will have first used versions of this tech with Snapchat filters, or equivalents on Facebook/Meta Messenger.

The Snapchat company have released a desktop version of these filters called Snap Camera, and they can be used with your webcam to add filters, masks, props or virtual avatars to your webcam view.

Snap Camera (or Snapcam for short) is a stand-alone programme, so if you wish to use it in Zoom, or other software, you'll need to change your camera source to Snap Camera. Just to quickly go over these steps:

Using Snap Camera with your video meeting software

Open Snap Camera and go up to the settings cog icon to select your camera input. Select your webcam, and you should see yourself come up on the screen.

In this application, you will be able to select from thousands of different filters and virtual masks and costumes that will be added to your camera view.

With Snap Camera running, now open your video meeting software, and select to change your camera source. From the available options you will see Snap Camera. Choose it and you will now have the filter for everyone in the show and audience to see.

Alternatives to Snap Camera

There are many alternatives to using Snap Camera available.

Zoom have introduced avatars which are virtual characters that track your movement. These are available from the Background and Effects menu in Zoom.

A popular one that I have personally used a fair bit in the past is called Facerig, but it has now been replaced by an updated version called Animaze. This software allows you to be replaced by fully rendered CGI characters like wolves, cats, pandas, dragons and human avatars as well.

Should you use virtual avatars in shows?

That is a choice that is firstly up to the director, and then up to you. If the director of the virtual show doesn't think this kind of thing fits with what they are trying to achieve on the show, then don't use them.

If the type of show is an improv show, or children's theatre show it may work well to use them. They can be great fun, but they can also create challenges.

Virtual characters are attention grabbing and therefore can distract from the story or take focus away from other performers. Sometimes it will be harmless to use an avatar but sometimes other performers may not like it. This doesn't mean you shouldn't ever use them, but it's about give and take. If there is concern about using them, check in with whoever is director or host of the show so see if they're OK with them being used or not.

The likeliness is that the technology for virtual avatars will only improve greatly in the next few years, and are likely to become very commonplace in online videos.

Voicemod

It is an application you can download for your computer and is to a microphone what Snap Camera is to your webcam. Voicemod allows you to add filters to manipulate your voice in a variety of ways.

You can make your voice sound like robots, aliens, hamsters, and such like. You can make it so that your voice echoes or sounds underwater. The app also allowed you to use sound effects form a soundboard.

When you have Voicemod set up, you'll need to select it as your microphone input in your video meeting software so the other performers can hear you. If you are also the person streaming the show you may have to add Voicemod as your mic source in your broadcasting software.

Like with virtual avatars, some people may find voice filters distracting. It would be best to talk to the director to decide if these are acceptable for the show or not.

Autocues and can/should you read your lines?

If you're performing in a virtual theatre show where you have scripted dialogue, you have a few options of how you tackle the task of learning lines.

Other than rare exceptions, stage actors with scripted dialogue will have to learn their lines. Film/Television actors usually learn their lines, although cue cards are used on rare occasions. Radio actors will familiarise themselves with their lines, but usually won't learn them, as they can read them without being seen by the audience.

So where does this put virtual theatre performers? Virtual theatre actors are shown on screen, but for the most part, the performers tend to appear in mid and close-up shots. You may just see their heads and shoulders, and sometimes their upper bodies, but rarely more than this.

In theory virtual theatre performers absolutely could have their scripts in hand or use cue cards or an autocue. You'd need to practice your technique to make sure it's not obvious you're reading.

Performers will still need to lift the dialogue up off the page and can't just keep their heads down to read the script in hand. Creative positioning of the script so it is out of shot, or reading lines off your laptop screen could give the illusion that you know your lines, but you need to question how noticeable this would be.

An autocue is a piece of equipment which is most commonly used by presenters who want to give the impression that they are talking directly to the audience at home. It allows them to look directly into the camera and deliver lines as they are reading. Setting one up to work with a webcam wouldn't be too difficult, but they come at a cost, and it would mean that the performer would always have to look directly into the camera to say their lines. This may be OK but may not be right for every show.

I would recommend a combination of the above techniques for most people. Virtual theatre is a new concept, and people have been very forgiving of some of its quirks and limitations so far. Many audience members will accept that a virtual theatre show online may feel like a play reading rather than a full-scale production. That isn't to say that performers can be lazy and just not learn their lines, but realistically the expectation is different and there are other ways to approach this.

Some people have multiple screens, and if you do, you could have your script displayed on each screen to give yourself different eyelines. Or if you have a script on a mobile phone or tablet, you could keep this handheld close to the webcam, but out of shot. That way you could give the illusion that you are almost looking at the camera when you are not. Cue cards could be placed strategically to create various eyelines.

Speaking of eyelines...

Adapting your performance style to work in virtual theatre shows

We've gone over many of the tech things a performer must consider when performing virtual theatre, but what about changes to your physicality, or vocal technique? Let's go over considerations for how to give the best performance for the medium of online shows.

Where should I look? Understanding eyelines in virtual theatre

First of all, if you don't know, your eyeline is where you are looking whilst performing. It enables the audience to understand where and who you are looking at. With virtual theatre, this is a problematic challenge for actors to overcome.

If you are the host/Emcee of a show, then by all means you should look directly into the camera when addressing the audience. It will give the audience the sense that you are talking to them.

If you are acting in a scene with one other actor, you have to decide where you look. The natural thing for you to do is look at your computer monitor, at the face of the other performer. That way you can see their expressions and react to exactly what they are doing. This makes sense, but it has a couple of issues to consider.

Firstly, I'll assume that your camera is positioned at the top of your monitor. Whilst this will give you good results, the audience may still get the sense that you're looking down slightly. They'll understand that you're looking at the other performer, but doesn't change that your eyes are still slightly down.

The second issue is that if every performer is looking at their screens, it means that there is little visual variety in the show. It would be like if a film only used one type of camera angle.

What can you do?

The best way to tackle this is to use your acting skills. Remember that you don't always have to be looking directly at someone when you're talking to them. You can intentionally look away from your screen at times to help convey the emotion or status of your character.

A character may look away and avoid eye contact if the character is afraid, or they may not look at the other person if they're self-obsessed. You may also find reasons to look away if they have a prop that they're interacting with. Variety will help keep the show visually interesting, and it will also make when you do look directly into the camera more intense or intimate.

Generally, I'd avoid putting my back completely to my camera as you can't really monitor if you're still in shot, and you voice may not be picked up by your mic as well.

Should actors simulate looking at each other by turning their heads to one side?

As mentioned above, most actors will naturally look to their screens to see the other actor's faces and reactions so they can respond to it. But the view for the audience is that the actors are all facing their screens for most of the time. In a film or TV show, we'd expect the actors to face each other.

You can achieve this effect by turning your head/body so that it creates the onscreen illusion for the audience that the characters are in the same room and facing each other. The big problem with doing this is that if you do this, you probably won't be able to see your screen and react to the other performer as well.

Another issue is that it is possible that a performer may think they are turned to face the other actor, and they may in fact be facing the exact opposite direction. This happens when some software doesn't display the participants in the same order on everyone's screens.

If you have multiple monitors, you could set things up to display the video call on each monitor. This would allow you to see the screen with your head turned in either direction. This will be more elaborate than most may want to bother with but is a viable solution.

What about scenes with three or more performers?

Things get trickier when there are three or more performers in a scene. Some video meetings will allow you to crop people's camera views so that you can have more people lined up side by side on the screen, but most will put people into stacked rows.

If you're in a scene and there are four people in it, it is very likely that you'll be stacked up two on top of the other two. If you have nine, you will end up with three rows of three. This can make realistic eye lines impossible.

It doesn't benefit online shows to have huge amounts of characters in a scene at the same time, but if you are in one, I would suggest turning your head in the direction towards the person you are talking to in a group scene. If everyone does this, the audience will be able to connect the dots and it will help them understand who is talking to who.

Unless you're scripted not to do so, using character names to identify who you are talking to will help things. You may also choose to display onscreen character or actor names that will be in the corner of each performer's webcam view. This will further help clarify who is who.

If you're onscreen always keep acting and reacting

If you're in a scene, and it isn't your line, you can still enhance the scene by reacting to what is going on with the other characters. Be an active listener and engage with what is going on. If the audience look at you and you look bored, and have your head down for no reason, it will take away from the work the other actors are doing in the scene.

Be a supportive performer/audience member

Depending on the type of show you are doing, a performer in a virtual theatre show may also need to take on the role of an audience member. It is possible to have actual audience members in a video meeting, and if the audio is set up to allow it, you may be able to hear them laugh or respond.

I would suggest not to do this, as audience members may intentionally or unintentionally hijack the show, or their volume may override that of the performers.

But what if you have a stand-up comedy show, improv show, magic show, or variety style show where it is acceptable and beneficial for there to be laughter or clapping and cheering at times?

I would recommend that any performers in the show all agree and have the understanding that they can add to the sense of atmosphere by laughing or clapping and cheering at appropriate times. This isn't to say to do fake laughs, or pretend things are funny when they aren't, but laughter is infectious. A supportive laugh will encourage a real laugh, and if you all respond positively to each other on the show, it will translate positively to the audience at home as well.

Sharing a scene and listening

If you're in a scene with one or several people, one of the first things you will have to get used to when performing in virtual shows is how to share the scene. There is a very slight time delay in the video calls and it can be very easy for performers to talk over each other, especially in chat or improv based shows.

If you really listen to each other, you'll be able to better judge when there are spaces to talk up or interject in conversations. Try to avoid talking over people to overpower their volume, as it will just create a wall of noise for the audience and probably lose the sense of harmony among the performers.

A good tip is to allow space for others to come in. You will quickly find that you all need to work together to get used to the time delay and not talking over each other. If you've been talking a lot, pass the baton to someone else to take over and then hopefully they'll do this back. If you find in an improvisation heavy show that this isn't happening, just raise it as something that everyone can work on to be better for next time.

Should I stand or sit whilst performing?

The answer to this will be party dictated by the space you have available, but will also be down to preference. Some performers are naturally very physical and will find the freedom of being able to move about will help with their character work and performance. If you fall into this category, it will be worth noting that you will still need to be aware of making sure you are in the frame and can be heard clearly.

Also, if you are very physical you will want to be careful of any potential hazards in your environment. If you are running around on a streaming show and trip and fall everyone will be able to see it happen, but no one will be there to provide immediate help. So be sensible!

Many people prefer to sit whilst performing in virtual shows. For the most part only a performers upper body will be seen anyway, and if you need to access your keyboard and mouse to access controls, it may make sense for you to be sat comfortably to use them.

If you are sat, you can still give a sense of walking, running, or other physical actions through movement of your upper body. This takes a little practice, but you can quickly find what works for you.

Physicality and miming

A limitation of virtual theatre is that the characters cannot physically interact with one another. Unless there are multiple performers in the same room, all sharing one webcam, there is no way for characters to physically hug, kiss, fight, hold hands, help each other up, or any of the million physical interactions that you can do in real life.

This means that as performers we need to be creative and use miming and dialogue to convey the same ideas. Physically leaning towards your camera and indicating that you want a hug will be understandable to the audience.

You can also do the same for a kiss, but unless you're going for a purposely gross out lips to the camera moment, a lean in and peck of the cheek off camera may be the best you can achieve.

Generally, I would expect performers to mime interactions with large physical objects or environments. So, pretending to turn a steering wheel will translate into the characters being in a car, and you can easily mime opening a door.

Try to make any mimes you do very clear, and if possible, use dialogue to support and confirm the actions you are doing physically. If you are in a scene where someone is doing a mime, give yourself enough time to understand what they are doing and see if there are things you can do to build upon these mimed actions.

If your mime and object work is clear, and you believe it, your audience will believe it too.

Props

If you are performing from your own home, the chances are that you will have easy access to a huge array of props that could come in handy for your virtual shows. Some virtual theatre shows will use a lot of props, and some will use none and instead mime everything. Many will use a combination of both, and I feel this is acceptable in many cases.

Audience members will understand if you pull out an actual cell phone to talk into, or grab a coffee cup for when a character is meant to be drinking. The same audience is unlikely to cry foul if you fail to materialise a hot air balloon for the end of the Wizard of Oz, and will understand that this had to be mimed.

Stage combat

Stage combat is a skillset that shouldn't be attempted by people who are not trained to do so. But virtual stage combat is likely to have limited risk. You always need to be aware of your surroundings if doing any physical performance, and I wouldn't suggest you attempt to do any roundhouse kicks towards your webcam in case your break something.

You will probably be safe enough to throw a pulled punch towards your webcam without going so far as actually smashing your laptop screen. The more creative out there may find several different attacks with armed or hand to hand combat that can look effective in virtual theatre. I'd only go as far as to suggest a few hand-based gestures such a punches and slaps, and maybe an elbow or headbutt as the limit of what will convey a fight to the audience.

If you play the character getting hit, just remember to react to the hits that you are given and maybe practice this lots before you put it into any show, so you can negotiate reactions and any issues from time delays.

Have fun with the limitations

I've given lots of serious advice up to this point, but there is an important thing to consider when performing in a virtual theatre show such as a play, musical, or improv...

It's pretty ridiculous!

Acting in general is a fun and kinda ridiculous concept. People pretending to be others and acting as if things are happening that really aren't. That's acting. I don't say this to knock anyone who loves acting because I love it too, but there is a reason why a play is called a play and that's because it's people playing!

Virtual theatre just happens to be that extra bit more ridiculous as we're now pretending we're in the same room when we aren't, and we'll sit in front of our computers for hours creating stories with people we may not have ever met.

The reason I say all of this is because people love to suspend their disbelief. Everyone can see virtual theatre has more barriers to suspending their disbelief than other forms of theatre or film, so there are ways we can have fun with this.

If it's appropriate for your show, a nod and a wink to the mechanics of a virtual theatre show are usually quite fun.

You can play with attempting to hand someone a physical object, and the audience will understand there is no actual way for the object to be taken by the other actor. It's silly, but it's fun.

You can play with physicality and enter the view of your webcam from the side or bottom, and people will understand that you've done this deliberately to take advantage of the fixed camera.

You can create illusions of your own hand entering the screen to throttle yourself as if it were someone else's arm.

You can purposely mute and unmute yourself at opportune moments, or mime talking to joke that you've been accidentally muted when you haven't.

There are loads and loads of fun things you can do to play with the restrictions and format of performing on a virtual theatre show. The only real limit here is your imagination.

24: COMBINING VIRTUAL THEATRE WITH IN REAL LIFE THEATRE

Virtual Theatre may have risen to prominence out of necessity and the limits of the COVID-19 lockdowns, but now people have discovered it, there are companies everywhere who are integrating it with in real life performances.

For many, this is as simple as live streaming an in real life show onto social media platforms, and for some, this is an opportunity to sell tickets to watch live streams of shows from theatres. Doing either of these certainly can increase audience awareness of your show or company, and this can be good for marketing. With this comes risks however, as a live stream of a theatre show may not fully translate the theatre experience to a screen.

Unless you have a multi camera set up, and good mics to ensure the cast can be heard well, you may find that the atmosphere of a live theatre show viewed online loses a lot in translation.

Another consideration is that the lighting design for a live theatre show may not work well onto a webcam, and you'll probably need expensive film or DSLR cameras with adjustable settings for lighting and focus to do justice to the stage experience.

But now let's get a bit more positive!

Technology is constantly improving and having multiple cameras and strong internet to stream a live theatre show is more accessible than ever. If you want to do this, then that is great. As the full technical setup for this could be the subject of a book in itself, I'll focus more on what is possible from a virtual theatre standpoint.

I'm talking about hybrid shows.

What if you designed a stage show where some of the performers were in different locations? Imagine a show that was happening in five different theatres that were in five different countries...and they were happening at the same time. Some of the scenes could feature the cast from the other theatres over a video link up displayed on a projection.

How cool would that be?

Yes, there would be a lot of logistics of time zones and making sure the internet didn't cut out, but it's something that is possible and within the grasp of even lower budgets now.

I'll leave this idea as food for thought for anyone creative who wants to tackle such a challenge, but it's the kind of show that is possible now.

But there are more ways to create hybrid shows

Even before the pandemic began, I would include live streaming elements in Extreme Improv shows to connect with audiences around the world. I started our show at the Alaska State Improv Festival with my mobile phone in hand and introduced the Alaskan audience to the Extreme Improv fans in the UK via a live stream on Facebook.

With what we have learned from virtual theatre, you could have audience suggestions in improv shows come from anywhere in the world, or guest performers join on screens. You could even have performers exit a theatre and continue the show outside, streaming what they're doing in real life locations back into the theatre.

25: THE FUTURE

Now that the concepts of virtual theatre performances have been unleased onto the world, it will be something that will only continue to develop and improve with time. The technology to do shows of this type existed before the COVID-19 pandemic, and necessity and innovation has brought it to the mainstream.

Whilst some predicted it would die out when the worst of the lockdowns were lifted, I predicted a rubber band effect. The amount of people creating or flirting with virtual theatre during the pandemic was huge and was like a stretched rubber band. When lockdowns began to lift, it was like the rubber band was released, and whereas it had been stretched wide with many people doing it, the amount has decreased dramatically to the point that the rubber band now looks very narrow indeed.

But a rubber band is springy, and like a rubber band, I expect that the initial snap of people backing away from virtual theatre will bounce back and forth until it finds a new normal position. It may not be stretched as wide as it was before, but many people who initially dropped doing it when lockdowns ended will return in time.

As innovation and technology improves, I expect within time that virtual theatre will sit alongside in person theatre, film, radio and any other kind of performance style as an equal.

I am excited for the future of virtual theatre and recognise that those who innovated out of necessity were the pioneers of a new form of performing arts. I'd like to think that I was part of that, and hope that this book is another step towards making virtual theatre accessible for everyone to create, perform and enjoy.

As some bold predictions for how virtual theatre will develop in the future, here are some thoughts. We can all laugh at them if you're reading this book several years after its publication and see that I was completely wrong. Or maybe I'll have a few things right and you'll nod your head at my predictions. Anyway, here goes...

Full body virtual avatars

We currently have face tracking which allows us to add virtual hats, hair and masks to our faces, but I see this developing much further.

I predict that in the future, we'll have full limb and body tracking integrated into video meeting software so we can have full virtual avatars. The technology for this is already out there and used by Hollywood movie studios through motion capture software and mocap suits, but I think it won't be long until we have it on every computer and smart device.

At the moment, our cameras mostly just capture our upper body and heads in virtual shows. I can see that in the future, cameras may be able to capture a wider view for the purposes of body tracking. This way you'll be able to display a close-up to the audience, but the camera could take in more data and know how the rest of your body is positioned outside the shot.

Alternatively, it may be that motion capture software will be able to better predict our body pose and fill in the blanks if a camera cannot fully see us.

Virtual props

A big addition of full body motion tracking will be virtual props. Currently I cannot hand a prop to another performer in a virtual show as we aren't in the same room. Yes, we can mime a prop to give this effect, but I think we'll be able to have virtual props that will stick to our hands, and can be passed from one virtual avatar to another. This will involve what is known as collision detection and is how video game characters know if they run into another character or something in their environment.

Virtual sets will become a thing

At least one of the video meeting software have already introduced 360 virtual backgrounds that move as you move your camera. Other video meeting software have introduced immersive or room view to give a sense that the meeting participants are all in the same physical location.

I predict that this will develop and within time we'll be able to have virtual sets which have a 3D sense to them. This may be like having a video game style 3D environment that allows for camera or lighting changes.

Virtual theatre will combine with virtual reality technologies to create a new kind of cinematic experience

This is already happening to a degree. People can meet virtually by wearing VR headsets and interact with others in virtual spaces. One big thing missing from this is that there aren't virtual camera operators to broadcast these interactions like a show.

Imagine if there was someone who could control a virtual camera crew to film these VR meetings from within the virtual world, and that what was being shot by the crew could be broadcast like any current streaming show.

This would mean people could watch the interactions like any 2D movie on their TVs, computers, and phones. Viewing these type of VR virtual shows wouldn't just be limited to people watching from within the same virtual reality space whilst also wearing a VR headset. These kinds of virtual shows could have camera angle changes, and basically anything that can be achieved in a real-world movie shoot.

26: AFTERWORD

And Boom! We're off the air!... Is usually the last words I will say to end a virtual theatre show. I'll say as the last thing the audience will hear, so technically I am not off the air until after I've said it, but it's a nice way to signal that the show is over.

I really hope you've found this book useful, and are excited to get going or dig deeper into your virtual theatre journey. For me, writing this book has been so much fun...at times, and a real challenge at times as well.

When I started writing it, I said to myself that I was going to avoid writing anything like a step-by-step guide to using any particular software. I knew applications will get updates and change. I hoped the book would be instead just full of ideas and concepts for people to experiment with. But after a few days' work I realised that if I didn't give step-by-step guides, who else would?

Sure, you can find guides on how to do anything on YouTube, but they're not tailored with virtual theatre in mind. I do plan to make videos to show how to do the things we've covered as a YouTube series. This will complement the book and help people see how things are done, so check them out on the Extreme Improv YouTube channel.

But I also know that sometimes having to watch a 20-minute tutorial video just to see if it explains how to do that thing that you're not really sure how to describe...can be super frustrating!

So, I figured screw it! I'll write a guide and tell you how to use the software I use. And once that was done, I thought people may feel disappointed if they already use a different software and this guide only covered an alternative.

Screw it again, I figured I'd write a guide for every piece of software I could think to use, even if it's not the best or ideal for the task of creating virtual theatre.

In this sense I felt a bit like Forest Gump who started running and when he got to the end of one street, he figured he'd just run to the next one, and then the next state and then the ocean...

So, I really hope that you've found this useful. I've tried to cover everything from the equipment needed, to how to use the software, through to designing your shows, performing on them, marketing your shows, and avoiding legal issues. If there's something I've not covered...well damn. My bad.

A funny thing is that this wasn't intended to be my second book. I've got two other books I'm currently writing, and each new one has been seen through farther into production than the last one. But since I'm writing the afterword of this one now, I guess this one will cross the finish line first.

It's time to wrap this up! So, until next time, don't forget to smash that subscribe button on youtube.com/extremeimprov, stay safe and always stay XStreamed!

And boom! We're off the air!

27: ACKNOWLEDGMENTS

I'd like to thank everyone who has been supportive of me and my work over the years. For my lovely girlfriend Rachel, with whom I would launch into random improv scenes whilst on holiday with a smartphone in hand to film us, these were our first virtual theatre scenes. You motivate me to keep creative and are a Ray of Adventure in my life. You did a fantastic job to help proofread my first book, and hopefully I've not made as many mistakes between 'then' and 'than' and 'form' and 'from' in this one because of you. Thank you for checking over this book where I made less mistakes then last time…

My parents Philip and Jane have always been so supportive of me pursuing my creative ambitions. Thank you for listening to me rattle on about all kinds of acting, filming or other technical things over the years. This all really helped me figure a lot of the stuff out that I do in my shows.

Thank you to Sarah and Eve, my sisters who have always been supportive of my shows. Thank you for sharing the shows and giving suggestions, be it feedback for the shows or suggestions for improv scenes in the audience.

And thank you to my niece Sophie. You're only two years old, but your understanding of how to watch Paw Patrol on a tablet gives me great hope that virtual theatre will become the norm for your generation.

Thank you Buddy and Rocky. Buddy is an amazing little Cavalier King Charles Spaniel and his name being Buddy is a great fit for such a good friend. And Rocky is a wonderful little pup. A lovely Working Cocker Spaniel who is cuddly and bouncy in equal measure!

I'd also like to thank all the other pet members of my family who have been great throughout my life. From my first pet gerbil Bingo Baby He-Man (I was three so that was his name), and my other gerbil pals Toaster, Mrs, and Super B, to my hamster chums Rusty, Toffee, Dusty, Sandy and April. Also my birdie friends Aussie, Magic, Freddie, Ellie, Mickey, Nipper, Ozzie and Sparky and the random pets like all the fish, Aqua Dragons, Sea Monkeys, Stick Insects and the random frogs that populated our pond. And lastly from the Pustansky animal kingdom, I'll give thanks to Chunky, Holly, Lucy and Tiny, the incredible King Charles Cavalier Spaniels.

Thank you to everyone who has been supportive of me and Extreme Improv and appeared live on stage, or on the virtual stage with me over the years. I've worked with countless brilliant performers who I have laughed and enjoyed performing with so much.

And thank you to the audiences who have watched the shows, subscribed on YouTube, bought this or my other books, and helped motivate and encourage me to keep pursuing what I love to do. I look forward to whatever is next and hope you will continue to follow what I do, and we can have more fun together!

28: MORE FROM EXTREME IMPROV

BOOKS

Extreme Improv Big Book of Improv Games

Extreme Improv Ultimate Guide to Creating Virtual Theatre

The Evolution of Video Game Controllers

BOARD/CARD GAMES

Extreme Improv: Improvise Your Way Outta This

Extreme Improv XStreamed Suggestion Cards

For info on all the fun stuff from Extreme Improv Xstreamed, please visit our website at www.xstreamed.tv

David Pustansky

www.ingramcontent.com/pod-product-compliance
Lightning Source LLC
Chambersburg PA
CBHW051510030726
47592CB00006B/2202